Contemporary Discourse
in the Field of
PHYSICS™

Gravitational, Electric, and Magnetic Forces

An Anthology of Current Thought

Edited by L.C. Krysac, Ph.D.

The Rosen Publishing Group, Inc., New York

This book is dedicated to the young people who have not yet ceased to question, and to those educators who keep those minds nurtured so that the questions continue to bloom.

Published in 2006 by The Rosen Publishing Group, Inc.
29 East 21st Street, New York, NY 10010

Library of Congress Cataloging-in-Publication Data

Gravitational, electric, and magnetic forces: an anthology of current thought/edited by L. C. Krysac.—1st ed.
    p. cm.—(Contemporary discourse in the field of physics)
Includes bibliographical references and index.
ISBN 1-4042-0405-9 (lib. bdg.)
1. Electromagnetism. 2. Gravity. I. Krysac, L. C. II. Series.
QC760.25.G73 2006
537—dc22

                                                    2004028904

Manufactured in the United States of America

On the cover (clockwise from top right): Patterns of light on a white surface; computer model representing the flow of electrons through a two-dimensional electron gas (2DEG); portrait of Sir Issac Newton; liquid crystal.

CONTENTS

Introduction   **5**

1. The Fundamental Properties of Electromagnetism   **10**

"Fraction Man" by Martin Perl   11

"Ghost in the Machine" by Bruce Schechter   20

From "Imaging Electron Flow" by Mark A. Topinka, Ph.D., Robert M. Westervelt, and Eric J. Heller   29

2. Applications of Electromagnetism and Electromagnetic Forces   **40**

From "What's Wrong with the Electric Grid?" by Eric J. Lerner   41

From "Supercapacitors Boost the Fuel Cell Car" by Fritz Gassmann, Rüdiger Kötz, and Alexander Wokaun   51

"Electrodynamic Tethers in Space" by Enrico Lorenzini and Juan Sanmartín   61

3. Electromagnetic Forces Applied in Scientific Research   **74**

"Magnetic Field Nanosensors" by Stuart A. Solin   75

From "Tiny Tips Probe Nanotechnology" by Ineke Malsch   90

From "Optically Trapped Fermi Gases" by John E. Thomas and Michael E. Gehm   97

From "The Little Machines That Are Making It Big" by David Bishop, Peter Gammel, and C. Randy Giles   109

4. Current Research on Electromagnetism 119

From "The Path to Ubiquitous and Low-Cost
  Organic Electronic Appliances on Plastic"
  by Stephen R. Forrest 120
"The Biggest Jolt to Power Since Franklin Flew
  His Kite" by Barnaby J. Feder 132
From "Diamagnetic Levitation" by Ronald E. Pelrine 137
From "Dusty Plasmas in the Laboratory, Industry, and
  Space" by Robert L. Merlino and John A. Goree 146

5. Gravitational Force on a Human Scale 159

"New Satellites to Map Gravity" by Warren E. Leary 160
"Free from Gravity, These Students Taste Outer
  Space" by John Schwartz 165
From "Searching for Gravity's Hidden Strength"
  by Jonathan L. Feng 173

6. Gravity and Cosmology 179

From "Gravitational Waves and the Effort to Detect
  Them" by Peter S. Shawhan 180
From "Gravitational Lenses" by Leon V. E. Koopmans
  and Roger D. Blandford 189

Web Sites 199
For Further Reading 200
Bibliography 201
Index 204

Introduction

Wherever you may be sitting, you are probably surrounded by a web of intricate electronic wiring through which a pulsing current of charge is flowing. The simple applications of electromagnetism that we have long come to take for granted are probably a finger's touch away from you turning them on or off: the lamp on your desk, the stove heating your meal, the heater warming the room, or the motor running to blow the air through the ducts. Other more complicated applications may be near you if, for example, you are one of the millions of people in the world who possess a computer. Computer systems rapidly exchange information via a combination of wireless, wired, and optical methods. Other applications of electromagnetism that you may have had contact with include cellular phones, automobiles, radar, radio and television broadcasting, digital photography, DVDs, and CDs. The list could be made much longer. The very basis of our technological society comes from the fundamentals of electricity and magnetism. The application of electromagnetism begins with simple charge flow, circuits, and motors, continues in the electronic wonders brought by the semiconductor and computing revolution, and moves forward with research that promises new technologies, such as electronic circuits from organic materials.

As you read the articles in this collection, it is hoped that you learn that though the study of electromagnetism began in the 1800s, the fundamentals of this subject are a collection of vibrant, relevant phenomena. The concepts discussed in even the most basic textbooks are being used in new and exciting applications, or being examined with fresh eyes in the hopes of creating the possibility of new, imaginative technologies. At the same time, advanced electronics are still established from fundamental properties.

The discovery that electric charge is the cause of the electric force, and how this force decreases with the square of the distance separating two charges, was made through the works of several important historical figures from the 1700s: Benjamin Franklin, Joseph Priestly, Henry Cavendish, and Charles Coulomb. It was Charles Coulomb who in the 1780s made the direct measurement of this force that attracts or repulses charges, and the law now bears his name. Electricity and magnetism are closely linked, as it is the motion of charges that creates magnetic fields, and a magnetic field exerts a force on any moving charge. These ideas were discovered in the 1800s, through the experiments of Hans Christian Oersted, André-Marie Ampère, and Michael Faraday, and are still being used in such applications as the creation of electrical power for orbiting spacecraft.

At the start of the 1900s, the quantum nature of the universe on the scale of the microscopic was revealed. Around that time, in 1910, Robert Millikan's delicate oil drop experiments concluded that the charge on the electron is the indivisible quantum unit of charge, and now all textbooks teach that every charge possible is an integral multiple of the electron charge. Fractional charges do exist on the very tiny quarks that make up atomic nuclei, and experiments are now being carried out with the hope of measuring fractional charges for the first time.

Electromagnetic forces, including the Coulomb force, are considered fundamental features of our universe, and on the scale of the very small, the quantum nature of this force has been revealed. In 1948, H. B. G. Casimir and D. Polder predicted, using quantum mechanics, that the interaction force between walls of atoms would be different from the Coulomb interaction. The attraction and repulsion between atomic scaled objects is known as the Casimir force, and it has become an important manifestation of the electromagnetic force for very small technological applications, such as for the micro machines known as MEMS (microelectromechanical systems).

Today, the fundamentals of electromagnetism are the subject of research and innovation on the way current flows, the resistance of various materials to current, how charge is stored on capacitors, the storage and transport of electrical power, and the electrical properties of materials, for example. The invention of the transistor in the 1940s, and the subsequent revolution in electronics, which led to the modern computer, are not the last technological inventions that will change our lives; new ways of exploiting the peculiar properties of extremely cold atoms, or organic molecules, or magnetic materials, for example, are currently being explored by scientists and engineers.

The force of gravity is the other fundamental force that affects our lives directly. Gravity, of course, was discovered by no one, but it was first described by Newton's law of universal gravitation in 1687, in his book *Philosophiae Naturalis Principia Mathematica*, commonly referred to as *Principia*. This is another inverse square law, and it describes the force with which every particle in the universe attracts every other particle. Henry Cavendish first measured the magnitude of this force in 1789, by delicately balancing two spheres on a thin fiber and then measuring the deflection due to the gravitational attraction to another nearby object. This law of gravity has held up for hundreds of years. With it, we can predict the gravity near Earth's surface, the trajectories of satellites and spacecraft, and the apparent weightlessness of objects and people in orbiting or falling spacecraft. These all remain relevant to understanding space exploration and monitoring the large-scale structure of Earth.

However, recent theories of gravitation suggest that Newton's law may not hold up on very small scales, so ultrasensitive Cavendish-type experiments are being undertaken to test this theory in laboratories around the world. The results from these experiments may provide evidence for a universe with six or more dimensions, only three of which are evident to us. If that wasn't enough to excite our imaginations, consider what happens when gravity is applied as the curvature of space-time instead of a simple force. When large masses distort the space-time geometry, gravity waves and the distortion of passing light in a lens effect may result. Both of these effects may prove exciting and useful tools for astronomers seeking to understand the nature of our universe. *—LCK*

1

The Fundamental Properties of Electromagnetism

The charge on the electron is a fixed quantity that never changes, and all charges are integer multiples of that one basic charge. This is the standard dogma that every physics textbook states, the result of countless measurements beginning with the famous oil drop experiments of Robert Millikan in 1909. The same oil drop experiments have been standard in undergraduate laboratories around the world since then, the purpose of which are to confirm what we already know: charge is quantized in the fundamental unit of the charge on the electron.

The scientific process demands, however, that no single physics concept can ever be free from doubt or reexamination, and scientific truth remains a truth as long as there are no repeatable experiments that contradict it. With this in mind, there is a possibility that there may be charges that are a fraction of the charge on the electron. Current experiments are being carried out in a world-class laboratory, the Stanford Linear Accelerator Center, to search for these *fractional charges. But something as fundamental as the basic unit of charge is so important to physicists that if there is any doubt about the long-held assumptions concerning that charge, then experiments to test those assumptions are needed. Nobel Prize–winner Martin Perl has taken on the challenge and describes the quest for a fractional charge in this article. —LCK*

"Fraction Man"
by Martin Perl
New Scientist, **June 21, 2003**

Driving south on Interstate 280 from San Francisco towards Silicon Valley, you soon pass a long, low structure stretching off for nearly 3 kilometres into the foothills of the Santa Cruz Mountains. Visible in satellite photographs of the Bay Area, this curious building houses a machine that accelerates electrons to feed a vast particle collider at the end of the line. But not all experiments probing the nature of matter at the Stanford Linear Accelerator Center are on such a grand scale.

Tucked away in a small laboratory at SLAC is an experiment less than 2 metres tall. It's a modern-day version of a famous experiment carried out in 1909 by American physicist Robert Millikan to measure the electric charge on tiny oil drops. Millikan's original research showed that electric charge always comes in indivisible chunks, the smallest of which is the charge carried by an electron. But my group and I believe our experiment at

SLAC could reveal an arcane family of particles that possess a mere fraction of an electron's charge.

No one has ever seen particles with a fractional electric charge and most scientists deny they can exist on their own. The only elementary particles that physicists can isolate and study are electrically neutral, such as photons and neutrinos, or have the same size of electric charge as the electron. These include the positron, the antimatter partner of the electron, as well as its heavier relations, the muon and tau.

However, there is no reason why there shouldn't be fractional charges. No accepted theory in physics objects to their existence and we believe that the searches carried out so far may not have been sensitive enough to detect them. In fact, physicists believe the quarks that make up protons and neutrons have 1/3 or 2/3 of an electron's charge. And although fractional-charge experiments take particular care in looking for these values, no evidence for lone quarks has surfaced. Instead they always appear bound together in combinations to form particles that have either no electric charge or a multiple of the electron's charge. This uncertainty both nags at and sings a seductive song to physicists.

There are good reasons to heed this song. Not only would the discovery of stable particles with a fractional electric charge open a new field in particle physics, it would improve our theoretical models, which have often skirted around the issue of fractional charge. Such a finding might also answer some questions about the early universe. For example, if we discovered single quarks it would substantially change our understanding of the nucleus and the strong force. One day we might even find a technological use for fractional charges.

My team and I began the hunt about 10 years ago. And over the years we have had to build ever more sensitive equipment. But in many ways, the first search for fractional charge particles started with Millikan's experiment. To establish the smallest chunk of electric charge, Millikan peered through a microscope at a fine mist of charged oil droplets falling through air under the influence of gravity. Using a stopwatch, he timed individual drops as they fell between two metal plates and worked out their downward terminal velocity. Keeping his eye on the same drop, he switched on an electric field and watched the droplet rise towards a charged plate. To calculate the charge on the drop, he simply compared its upward and downward terminal velocities, the difference being proportional to the charge.

Millikan and his colleagues managed to measure hundreds of drops, but their approach was painstakingly slow: it took nearly an hour to prepare and select a suitable drop. Worse still, the measurements were made by hand and might have been prone to bias. So if signs of fractional electric charge had shown up, they might have been dismissed or even exaggerated.

All this makes Millikan's original approach unsuitable for searching for something as rare and mysterious as fractional electric charge. We needed to adapt the experiment so that it could analyse over 100 million oil drops and measure the charge of each in a fraction of a second. Twenty years ago, this would have been no more than a dream. But in the last decade, low-cost equipment from the personal computer industry has made our long-odds experiment possible. For example, to generate drops quickly and with the same diameter (6–25 micrometres), we use micro-machined ejectors based on ink-jet printer technology. And we have replaced Millikan's tedious observation and hand-recording of the drops with an automated imaging system that uses CCD cameras connected to powerful computers. Even the data we generate, which runs to gigabytes per week, would have cost a fortune to store and analyse before the advent of cheap hard drives, CD-ROMs, and DVDs.

To make our measurements as accurate as possible, we wanted to measure each drop several times. This meant slowing the drops right down as they fell through the air. To do this we used a simple trick: we blew a steady stream of air upwards to cushion their fall. This involved rearranging the metal plates so they were vertical rather than horizontal as in Millikan's original set-up. If we hadn't done this, we would have had to punch holes in the metal plates to let the air through. This would have distorted the electric field acting on the drops, pulling them faster in certain directions and spoiling our calculations.

In our new set-up, we alternate the electric field between the plates so that as the drops fall, they wiggle from side to side. To calculate the charge, we measure the drops' terminal velocity in both directions and work out the difference, which is related to the charge. This has allowed my colleagues—Valerie Halyo, Peter Kim, Eric Lee, Irwin Lee, and Howard Rogers—and I to pin down the charge of each drop to an accuracy of about 1/30 of an electron charge.

So far we have measured 64 million droplets of silicone oil and found no evidence of fractional charge. In total we have searched 90 milligrams of oil, which means there is less than one particle with a fractional charge for every ten thousand billion billion neutrons and protons. That is, fractional charge particles are extremely rare, at least in silicone oil.

But what about in other materials? While other groups in the US, Italy, and the UK have looked for fractional charges in niobium, mercury, and iron, they have hunted through a mere 16 milligrams of matter. Researchers have also hunted through cosmic rays and among the particle debris produced in accelerators. So far they have found nothing, but the results indicate that any fractional charge particle must be at least a hundred times heavier than a proton—otherwise accelerators would have found one.

With all these failures, maybe we should have given up on fractional charge particles several years ago. But we didn't quit. We couldn't help wondering if the previous searches had been looking in the wrong place. Oil, iron, and niobium are all processed materials, and the fractional charge particles may have been lost during processing. We reasoned it would be better to look in a raw material that had not been refined chemically or by other means.

We chose to look in meteoritic material from asteroids. If lone quarks or any other isolated fractional charges were created in the violent birth of the universe, they could have been incorporated into the planets and asteroids when the solar system formed 4.6 billion years ago.

Geological and chemical processes such as melting would have filtered these particles out of the Earth's surface, wiping out any trace of them on the planet. However, many of the meteorites landing on Earth were formed at the same time as the solar system and haven't undergone any refining. We believe meteorites called carbonaceous chondrites might contain fractional charge particles because they contain some of the most pristine material in the solar system. In particular we have been using samples from the famous Allende meteorite that fell in Mexico in 1969. Samples of Allende are plentiful and cheap, costing just a few dollars per milligram.

This isn't the first search for fractional charges in meteorites. In the early 1980s, Gareth Jones of Imperial College in London and his colleagues searched through samples of iron-nickel and stony meteorites and found nothing. But we think carbonaceous chondrites might be a better place to look because they are good electrical insulators. This means they might hold a fractional charge more securely in their mineral matrix than a good conductor such as iron.

A few years ago we began developing a way to suspend powdered meteorite in mineral oil and then make small droplets of the suspension. We grind the meteorite so that most of the particles are less than one micrometre across and mix the powder with oil. To that we add surfactant chemicals, which help keep the powder in suspension. In tests we found we were able to make drops about 25 micrometres in diameter and containing 2 to 4 percent meteorite. If any droplets contained stray fractional charges, they would then show up in our measurements.

Things seemed to be going well, but then we hit problems. First we found that the oil-meteorite drops carry charges hundreds and thousands of times the charge of a single electron—far greater than the charge on pure silicone oil droplets, which somehow avoid becoming ionised due to friction as they pass through air. This is a problem because it makes it far harder to pin down the accuracy of the measured charge on the drops. The total charge affects the precision with which we can measure the terminal velocity of the drop, and this uncertainty feeds into our calculation. Instead it is far better to use droplets carrying up to just 10 times the charge of an electron. We solved this by passing the droplets through highly ionised air, which neutralises excess ions in the oil drops and lowers their charge.

A much more serious problem was that making uniform droplets from oil-meteorite suspension every day is much more difficult than making uniform droplets of pure oil. The larger particles in the meteorite powder gradually settle above the hole through which the drops are sprayed. Eventually the hole becomes completely clogged and the spray stops working. To get round this we have to remix the suspension and adjust the spray—

it is quick to fix but an annoying interruption. Once again we thought of quitting.

However, the concept of fractional charge particles continued to seduce us and we have persevered. We have found that with patience we can operate the drop generator and collect data for several days at a time. What's more, we are designing a feedback system that senses changes in the drops' properties and adjusts the operating conditions to match.

So far we have searched through less than a milligram of the carbonaceous chondrite meteorite without any sign of fractional charges, but our goal is to study several milligrams. We even dream of searching through 100 milligrams of meteorite, but we don't yet know how to accomplish this. Perhaps this dream may have to be left to the next generation of physicists who heed the seductive song of fractional charge particles.

At present, to my knowledge, we are the only researchers looking for fractional charge particles in matter. Those people who used to hunt for them now work in other areas. That's because most experiments today look for things theorists say ought to exist. No theories call for, or even hinge on, the existence of fractional charge particles roaming freely around the universe. But we believe the scientific pay-off of finding something totally new and unexpected is worth it.

Reprinted with permission from *New Scientist*

Are there any basic physics ideas that can be indisputably free from doubt and criticism? The answer is no, since the basic cornerstone of the scientific method is that any theory is only as good as the experiments supporting it. As soon as any repeatable experiment produces results that contradict a theory, that theory needs careful revision if not outright abandonment.

Recently, experiments have been producing results that contradict the predictions of long-standing theories that describe how electric current flows through metals. This development has puzzled physicists working hard to find the solution.

Writer Bruce Schechter has interviewed Philip Phillips, a professor of physics at the University of Illinois at Urbana-Champaign, and finds that electric current, something we all take for granted, isn't so easy to explain. Even in a simple copper wire carrying the current to your reading lamp, a fascinating dance of quantum waves and cooperating seas of electrons is taking place. The theories that describe this dance are contradicted in experiments performed at ultralow temperatures, where materials can be insulators, conductors, or superconductors. These and other concepts are briefly discussed, giving us a glimpse of the complexities of electric current. —LCK

"Ghost in the Machine"
by Bruce Schechter
New Scientist, May 29, 2004

You probably take it for granted, and why shouldn't you? Electrical conductivity, the ability of electrons to move virtually unimpeded through the dense thicket of atoms that comprise a chunk of metal, is surely one of the most familiar and useful things in your life. Discovered by Michael Faraday, who presciently declared that governments would one day tax it, it has now become the basis of almost all modern technology. Life without electricity flowing through metals is almost unimaginable now.

Well, don't worry—electrical conductivity isn't going away. But a growing number of physicists are realising that their understanding of conductivity is on shaky ground, to say the least. "The conventional theory of metals is in crisis," says Philip Phillips, a professor of physics at the University of Illinois at Urbana-Champaign. Given how long we have thought we understood what makes metals metallic—it was an early triumph of quantum mechanics—this might seem silly. But Phillips isn't joking. "Things are really strange," he says. "We've never had a time like this before."

This crisis centres on a striking mismatch between theoretical predictions about the properties of conductors and the results of experiments designed to confirm those theories. So far the only way to resolve the mismatch is to invoke the existence of an entirely new state of matter, which would mean the existence of a new kind of metal. And though plenty of people have been looking, no one has yet found either the new state of matter or the new kind of metal.

Before 1928, the fact that a hunk of copper or iron conducted electricity at all was a deep mystery. The atoms in a metal are arranged in a stunningly regular crystalline lattice, and neighbouring atoms sit close enough together to be able to swap their outer electrons, which thus become liberated to form an "electron sea." But it was not clear how these electrons could travel any distance without colliding with the remaining densely packed atoms.

In 1928, the Swiss physicist Felix Bloch found the answer. According to quantum mechanics, electrons can behave like waves. He showed that if the electrons' wavelength matched the spacing of the atoms, they could surf through the lattice without any trouble.

Bloch considered perfect crystals, but in the real world crystals are pocked with defects. When the crystal forms, the atoms often fail to stack into a perfect lattice, rather like a display of oranges built by a careless grocer. Or the crystal might contain impurities, like lemons among the oranges. Nevertheless, physicists were confident that the electrons could adjust their wavelengths, and this would explain why defects and impurities don't destroy the conductivity of metals.

In 1979, the subject of defects and conductivity came under scrutiny again, this time from Philip Anderson, perhaps the greatest condensed matter physicist of his generation—and hot off winning his 1977 Nobel prize—along with Elihu Abrahams, T. V.

Ramakrishnan and Don Licciardello. The "gang of four," as they were called, looked at two-dimensional crystals, in which the electrons are essentially confined to move in just two dimensions, and considered what happens as they are cooled to absolute zero (from now on assume that we are talking about materials at absolute zero unless stated otherwise). Anderson calculated that even an extremely small number of defects would destroy a metal's conductivity.

That is because in two dimensions an electron wanders about the lattice like a drunk around a lamppost. The effect, now known as Anderson localisation, shows that eventually the drunk will stumble back to the lamppost. So an electron scattering off a defect will eventually find its way back to the defect: it becomes localised, or stuck in the lattice. Unless the metal is a perfect crystal, at absolute zero it should be an insulator in two dimensions. In other words, there are no two-dimensional metals.

Anderson's result provided a way to reduce things down to a place where we could test our fundamental theory of metals. It was based on mathematics so clear and elegant that it seemed it had to be right. However, when experimenters finally had the technology to check it they were in for a surprise. Using the techniques developed to manufacture semiconductors, physicists learned to experiment on very thin films. In 1994 Sergey Kravchenko and his collaborators at Northeastern University in Boston, Massachusetts, found that contrary to the theory, a thin film of silicon appeared to become a metal when cooled almost to absolute zero. Of course, it would be physically impossible for Kravchenko to cool his sample to precisely absolute zero, but he got to within thousandths of a degree, and extrapolating the results clearly indicated that the film would behave as a metal. The experiment has been refined and repeated over the years, and the effect has consistently appeared. Phillips says the results mean that theorists "have some explaining to do."

As is their wont, theorists have not been slow to concoct theories, but so far little consensus has emerged. Anderson localisation was based on what physicists call perturbation theory. The idea is to start from a theoretical perfect crystal, which you can analyse exactly, and then slowly add disorder to the crystal, either by disrupting the positions of the atoms or by adding impurities. For the Kravchenko experiments, it is also necessary to include the interactions between the electrons.

Critics say that this works fine for a small amount of disorder and electron interactions, but it becomes unwieldy and breaks down as the amount of disorder and electron interaction increases. They suggest that what is needed is an analysis that starts from a highly interacting state. But the perturbative theorists deny there is anything wrong with their techniques, and say that the experimenters' extrapolations are wrong: once they cool their films close enough to absolute zero they will see that they become insulators. Of course, you can't disprove this line of argument, since you can never reach absolute zero. "Welcome to hell," says physicist Gergely Zimanyi at the University of California, Davis.

The crisis in our understanding of conductivity would be bad enough if it were confined to metals. But there is also a problem with superconductors. The theory says that at absolute zero, two-dimensional superconducting films should either remain super-conducting or become insulators. But experiments done by Allen Goldman and his colleagues at the University of Minnesota in Minneapolis once again seem to contradict the theory: they indicate that these materials turn into metals.

In a superconductor, electrical charge is carried by electrons loosely bound into what are known as Cooper pairs. Electrons possess a quantum mechanical property called spin, analogous to the spin of a top. An electron possesses a spin of 1/2 (the units are Planck's constant divided by 2), and particles like this with "half-integer" spin are called fermions. In contrast, particles with integer spin such as photons, which have spin 1, are called bosons.

Quantum mechanics forbids any two fermions from sharing the same quantum state (which is why the electrons in atoms don't all simply collapse into a single orbit), but when two electrons form a Cooper pair, adding their spins means they effectively become a boson. And just as the boson nature of photons gives lasers their power, the boson nature of Cooper pairs is the secret behind the power of superconductivity. Where does the power come from? From the fact that bosons like to be in the same state.

The Cooper pairs of electrons all "condense" into the same quantum state, like a gas becoming a liquid. This

change creates order from chaos, allowing the pairs to move through the crystal like a well-rehearsed marching band. "They have the same phase," Phillips says. "When they march out of step, the result is an insulator."

In fact, the famous Heisenberg uncertainty principle says that those are the only two possibilities for this sea of bosons—insulating or superconducting. In its most familiar form, the uncertainty principle says that you cannot simultaneously measure the exact position and momentum of a particle; the more accurately you know one quantity, the more uncertain the other becomes. But in its most general form, the information trade-off of the uncertainty principle extends to any pair of what physicists call conjugate variables, such as energy and time.

In the case of a sea of particles, the phase and the particle number form a pair of conjugate variables. If the phase of the particles is known perfectly—that is, if the particles are all marching in lockstep as bosons can—then the number of particles is infinitely uncertain. "What that means is if you take snapshots of one region of a superconductor, you'll see that the particle number in the region you are looking at changes wildly," Phillips says.

A fluctuating particle number indicates a flow of electrons, just as a constantly changing number of leaves on the surface of a stream would indicate it was flowing. If the number of leaves you count in a section of stream remained fixed, you would conclude that the leaves were languishing on a stationary surface. A wildly fluctuating particle number is what gives a superconductor its zero resistance to the flow of electrons.

But if the particles fall out of lockstep and begin milling around like a marching band on a break, the phase becomes unknown, which means the particle number is known exactly. "The particle number is not fluctuating, which means they are not moving," Phillips says. So there can be only two states: superconducting or insulating.

So much for the theory. Experiments seem to indicate that—in direct contradiction to the uncertainty principle—superconductivity does indeed disappear at absolute zero and is replaced not by an insulator, but by a metallic state consisting of bosons.

Phillips and others have been struggling to reconcile the existence of these "Bose metals" with the uncertainty principle. As with the silicon film, which was predicted to become an insulator near absolute zero but in fact behaved like a metal, one approach is to simply say that the experiments cannot yet have got close enough to absolute zero. But others argue that the Cooper pairs that produce the superconductivity are embedded in a metal-like sea of electrons. At temperatures clear of absolute zero, they say, the superconducting Cooper pairs mask the material's metallic character by effectively short-circuiting it. As the material cools and the super-conductivity vanishes, as the uncertainty principle requires, the underlying metal is revealed.

Though this describes what is happening pretty well, it does not deal with the difficult question of how a material can be transformed from a metal to a superconductor, a question rather like asking how a material could be both a liquid and a solid.

Phillips's own explanation is that the bosons condense into a glass-like state. Unlike crystals, glasses are flowing, dynamic structures. The atoms in a glass have no overall order and no unique ground state, and slowly move by nudging each other aside. To explain how this leads to metallic behaviour, Phillips returns to the marching band analogy. Imagine that the band is marching up a very steep hill, and as the musicians tire at different rates, they fall out of step at different rates. "Although the whole band is out of step, there will be local regions of order where groups of musicians still march in step," Phillips says.

This is a state in which there is local order—pockets of musicians marching in step—but global disorder. It is a state that the conventional models of superconductivity have not considered. The phase (and therefore particle number) of this state is neither entirely unknown or completely certain, so the material is somewhere between a superconductor and an insulator: a metal.

There's still a long way to go before the crisis is properly resolved, but Phillips is optimistic; it could prove unexpectedly fruitful, he says. After all, even the smallest crisis can prefigure revolutionary changes. A tiny discrepancy between the observed orbit of the planet Mercury and that computed by Newton was eventually settled by Einstein's theory of gravity. All we need now is the Einstein of electricity.

Reprinted with permission from *New Scientist*

Semiconductor heterostructures, the basis of computer chips, can be found in much of the technology in which we are surrounded. Although a great deal is known about the physics of semiconductors, in the past there were no methods for visually imaging the way electrons flowed through these devices. Recently, some physicists have been taking a closer look at electron flow, in the hopes of obtaining greater understanding of semiconductor devices and perhaps then developing new technologies.

Mark Topinka, a postdoctoral fellow at Stanford University; Bob Westervelt, a professor of physics at Harvard University; and Eric Heller, a professor of physics and chemistry at Harvard University, review the tricky methods used to obtain images of electrons functioning inside semiconductors. In the world of the very small, the quantum regime, where the electrons move, small particles behave as probabilistic waves. Quite appropriately then, the arsenal of devices discussed takes advantage of quantum effects in and out of magnetic fields.

This article discusses, for example, how the champion of atomic microscopes, the scanning tunneling microscope (STM), can be used to visualize electron structures in a semiconductor by capacitive coupling techniques. All of the techniques discussed expand the reach of our vision beyond simple microscopes. —LCK

From "Imaging Electron Flow"
by Mark A. Topinka, Ph.D., Robert M. Westervelt, and Eric J. Heller
Physics Today, December 2003

Semiconductor heterostructures have revolutionized solid-state physics and its applications. Most of us use the fruits of this revolution every day in CD and DVD recorders and players, cellular telephones, laser-based telecommunications, satellite television, and much more. The technology, based on atomic layer-by-layer growth using molecular beam epitaxy (MBE), is sophisticated, remarkable, and marketable.

One class of semiconductor heterostructures, the two-dimensional electron gas (2DEG), has been a focal point for theorists and experimentalists and a wellspring of new physics. A 2DEG can be produced at low temperatures at an interface of two distinct layers (a so-called heterojunction) doped nearby with atoms that donate electrons. The electrons at such a junction are confined to the lowest quantum state in the direction normal to the interface; by charging gate electrodes on the top surface of the heterostructure some distance away to repel them, the electrons can be further confined in the other directions to make dots, wires, resonators, and other shapes. . . . The potential for exploiting these and many other quantum effects is spawning new fields of single electronics[3] and spintronics[4]—new approaches to logic that use single electron charges and spins to represent bits of data—and the new area of quantum information processing, based on the coherent interaction of quantum mechanical qubits.[5]

Despite all the beautiful experiments already performed on 2DEGs and all that is riding on the new science and phenomena made possible by them, researchers have been blind until recently as to how electrons actually move through them. Most of the knowledge of electron flow in 2DEGs is indirect, based on electron-transport measurements of macroscopically averaged quantities. To be sure, many of the statistical properties are known, such as the electron mean free path. But macroscopically averaged parameters do not reveal the details of the fascinating behavior to be found on the nanoscale. For that, imaging is needed.

Imaging a system is essential to understanding its fundamental properties and developing new electronic and magnetic devices. Imagine the difficulty of designing and fabricating an integrated circuit from a silicon crystal without the use of an optical or electron microscope.

As device sizes continue to decrease, quantum behavior becomes important and offers new research and application opportunities. To understand the fundamental behavior of electrons in this quantum regime and to make functioning devices based on this behavior, one must develop ways to visualize the flow of electron charges and spins through semiconductors. The invention of the scanning tunneling microscope (STM) allowed researchers to directly view the pattern of atoms on a material's surface. Additional methods are needed to image the flow of electrons beneath the surface.

Obtaining images of 2DEGs inside semiconductors is no easy matter, because the electrons are buried beneath the surface and because the samples must be cooled to low temperatures to show quantum behavior. Nonetheless, a number of groups have recently developed liquid-helium-cooled scanning probe microscopes (SPM) for this purpose.

Making a Two-Dimensional Electron Gas

Two-dimensional electron gases possess a unique combination of parameters that together make an ideal laboratory in which to explore the fascinating and often surprising behavior of such systems. . .

Because they do not collide often with other particles, the electrons have a long phase-coherence length—that is, they can travel coherently for many microns as quantum mechanical waves with a well-defined phase and with the same energy. They also have a long mean free path: Electrons can flow through a 2DEG for tens or even hundreds of microns before losing track of their initial direction. . .

Imaging the Quantum Hall Regime

The quantum Hall effect (QHE) profoundly changes the way electrons move through a 2DEG.[1] In a strong magnetic field applied perpendicular to the 2DEG, the electrons no longer travel as free plane waves but instead occupy a series of discrete Landau levels separated in energy. Motion along the field lines cannot occur, because the electron gas is two-dimensional. . .

The QHE is associated with remarkable spatial structures in the 2DEG. The structures include predicted spatially striped phases of the quantum Hall liquid that have been investigated using macroscopic measurements. Imaging the properties of a 2DEG in a strong magnetic field at low temperatures is a particularly useful way to understand the QHE, and a number of groups have developed cooled scanning probe microscopes for this purpose.

Raymond Ashoori's group at MIT has developed a way to image electron flow in the quantum Hall regime using a subsurface charge accumulation (SCA) probe.[6] An STM tip held above the surface capacitively couples to the 2DEG immediately below. When a small AC voltage is applied between the tip and the 2DEG, the resulting flow of charge in the gas induces an oscillating image charge on the tip; that oscillation is detected by a sensitive electrometer. Adding a positive DC voltage to the tip allows spatial profiling of the 2DEG by creating a small bubble composed of a few electron charges beneath the tip. The bubble is surrounded by an insulating ring of incompressible fluid in the quantum Hall regime, and it forms an electrically isolated quantum dot that holds a fixed, discrete number of electron charges.[7] . . .

Imaging Electron Flow in Low Magnetic Fields

Although many insights have come from imaging the quantum Hall regime, the majority of semiconductor devices operate without an applied magnetic field, making it important to image in that regime, too. Recent

imaging by our group at Harvard University, by Paul McEuen, by Charles Smith and David Ritchie at the University of Cambridge, and by Klaus Ensslin has focused on electron flow patterns in a 2DEG with no applied magnetic field or with small magnetic fields. Mark Eriksson, working with two of us (Topinka and Westervelt), led the charge in 1996 by directly imaging the mean free path in a 2DEG for electrons passing through a wide constriction.[13] Four years later, Rolf Crook and colleagues at Cambridge imaged cyclotron orbits in a 2DEG at 4.2 K and interpreted features of their images in terms of the deflections in electron trajectories caused by donor atom density fluctuations and impurities.[14] Using a charged atomic-force microscope tip to bend the trajectories of electrons traveling between two quantum point contacts (QPCs), they achieved glimpses into the spatial details of electron flow in 2DEG nanostructures. Those early experiments set the scene for more recent high-resolution images that revealed surprising and important details about electron flow in 2DEGs.

At Harvard, we used scanning probe microscopy to image the coherent flow of electron waves through a 2DEG with no applied magnetic field.[15, 16] We focused on the pattern of electron flow through one of the most fundamental and widely used nanostructures: a QPC,[17] a narrow constriction whose width is comparable to the electrons' Fermi wavelength λ_F. As its width is increased, the conductance of a QPC increases in steps of height $2e^2/h$ because the electrons travel through individual transverse modes, each of which contributes $2e^2/h$ to the total conductance.

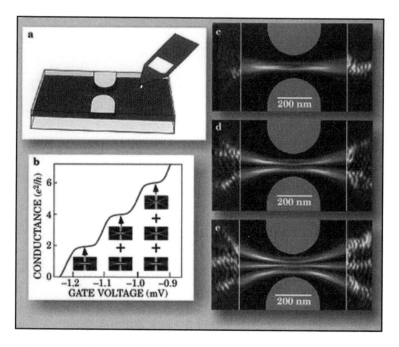

Figure 4: Electron flow through a quantum point contact. **(a)** Scheme for imaging current flow through a QPC using scanning probe microscopy. Two gate electrodes *(center)* create a narrow constriction in the underlying two-dimensional electron gas. A charged tip *(upper right)* depletes the electron gas below it, creating a divot *(white spot)* that scatters incoming electron waves, as shown in the simulations. **(b)** The conductance of the QPC, measured at 1.7 K, increases in quantized steps as the gate voltage (and QPC width) is increased. The insets below each step show simulations of the spatial pattern of electron flow for the transverse modes that contribute to the conductance. **(c–e)** Experimental images of electron flow at 1.7 K *(left and right)* and theoretical simulations *(center)* for the first three transverse modes of a QPC. The observed interference fringes spaced by half the Fermi wavelength demonstrate the coherence of electron flow. Because the additional flow, appearing as the QPC becomes wider, is due to the newly opened-up mode, the image for each transverse mode could be obtained by subtracting the raw images from the next lower step. *(Adapted from http://www.physicstoday.org/ pt/vol-56/iss-12/captions/p47cap4.shtml)*

Figure 4a illustrates our technique for imaging the flow of electron waves in a GaAs-AlGaAs 2DEG. Gates on the surface form a QPC whose width could be adjusted by changing the gate voltage. A charged SPM tip capacitively couples to the electron gas below; for negative tip-to-gas voltages, it can deplete a small, round divot in the 2DEG that reflects electron waves arriving from the QPC. The pattern of electron waves scattered by the divot under the tip is shown by theoretical simulations in the figure. Some of the electrons reflected by the divot return along their incoming path and travel back through the QPC, measurably reducing its conductance. Electrons scattered at other angles have little effect on the conductance because they remain on the same side of the QPC. The change in conductance induced by the tip is proportional to the flux of electrons hitting the divot under the tip. As the tip is scanned over the sample, the QPC conductance images the electron flux that was there before the tip was present.

With this technique, we could image the patterns of electron flow through the individual transverse modes of the QPC that are responsible for the conductance steps shown in figure 4b.[15] Figures 4c–e compare experimental images of the flow of electron waves through the first three modes of the QPC (outside), with theoretical simulations (inside). The spatial character of the modes is clearly visible: Electron flow through the first mode shows one angular lobe; flow through the second mode shows a V-shaped pattern with two angular lobes and a zero down the center; and flow through the third mode shows three angular lobes with two zeros. In addition, the experimental images show interference fringes, spaced by $\lambda_{F/2}$ (about 20 nm), that demonstrate that the flow of electron waves is quantum mechanically coherent over the imaged distances.

The spatial resolution of the images in figure 4 is excellent, considering the much larger size—about 100 nm across—of the divot of depleted electron gas. How can such great resolution occur? The tip must backscatter electrons arriving from the QPC in order to change the conductance and produce a signal. Imagine you are standing in a large room with black walls, holding a flashlight against one side of your head with its beam pointed forward. To sense the pattern of flow of light from the flashlight, a friend holds a silver ball in the light beam. Only a small glint of backscattered light, much smaller than the ball itself, will be visible to you. Similarly, the spatial resolution in images of electron flow is determined by the size of the glint, which is much smaller than the reflecting divot under the tip.

At greater distances from the QPC, we discovered that the electron flow formed remarkably narrow branches, as shown in figure 5 for the first QPC conductance step.[16] From the experimental images and simulations close to the QPC shown in figure 4c, one might expect to see a single broad angular lobe of flow in figure 5 for the first mode of the QPC. Instead, the electron flow forms narrow branches within distances from the QPC of much less than the electron mean free path, which is 11 μm for this sample. The branches in images of electron flow are reproducible as long as the

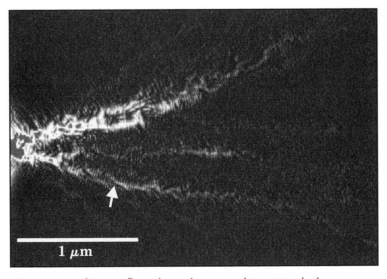

Figure 5: Electron flow through a two-dimensional electron gas from a quantum point contact on the first conductance step. The image shows surprisingly narrow branches that are produced by small-angle scattering from charged donor atoms in the donor layer. The interference fringes, demonstrating quantum mechanical coherence, extend throughout the image. The arrow points to a cusp produced by the focusing effect of a nearby impurity atom. (Adapted from http://www.physicstoday.org/pt/vol-56/iss-12/captions/p47cap5.shtml)

sample is kept at liquid-He temperatures. Fringes spaced by $\lambda_{F/2}$ are observed over the entire image; their presence again underscores the coherent wavelike nature of electron transport in 2DEGs over large distances at low temperatures. . .

. . . Ray-tracing simulations of the classical trajectories for electrons in an accurate depiction of the potential landscape in the 2DEG gives results like figure 6c, which shows a branching structure similar to the experiments.[16] . . .

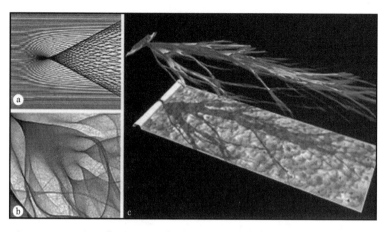

Figure 6: Simulations of electron flow. (a) Parallel electron trajectories, going from left to right, form a V-shaped cusp due to focusing by a potential-energy dip caused by a charged donor atom (not seen) above a two-dimensional electron gas. **(b)** A realistic 2DEG simulation that includes many ionized donors forms several generations of cusps. The electrons travel here from upper left to lower right. **(c)** Ray-tracing simulations of electron flux emerging from a small opening into a region of random potential reflect the features seen in experimental images of 2DEG quantum point contact samples. The potential is shown gray in the valleys and white on the peaks. The electron flux is coded by height and color, with dark gray corresponding to regions of low flux; still lower flux is transparent. The "shadow" of the flux on the potential plot shows where the flux lies relative to the hills and valleys; no guiding valleys are seen. A slight change of the position of the opening changes the location and direction of the branches. *(S. E. J. Shaw, Ph.D. thesis, Harvard University, 2002)*

The success that a number of groups have had in imaging the flow of electrons—the lightest by far of all the easily accessible particles—through a 2DEG involves a subtle change of mindset, away from the ensemble and toward the individual. In condensed matter physics, there is a strong tradition of considering ensemble averages, but now researchers are increasingly confronted with a specific quantum structure, with all its warts and bumps. For example, the branching of electron flow in 2DEGs is entirely consistent with earlier work using macroscopic measurements of conductance. But the newly discovered branches put a face on the real agent of momentum decorrelation and even tell where donor atoms may be located in a particular sample.

References

1. T. Chakraborty, P. Pietilain, eds., *The Quantum Hall Effects: Intergral and Fractional*, 2nd ed., Springer-Verlag, New York (1995).

3. K. K. Likharev, *Proc. IEEE* **87**, 606 (1999) [INSPEC].

4. S. A. Wolf, D. D. Awschalom, R. A. Buhrman, J. M. Daughton, S. von Molnar, M. L. Roukes, A. Y. Chtchelkanova, D. M. Treger, *Science* **294**, 1488 (2001).

5. C. H. Bennett, D. P. DiVincenzo, *Nature* **404**, 247 (2000) [INSPEC].

6. S. H. Tessmer, P. I. Glicofridis, R. C. Ashoori, L. S. Levitov, M. R. Melloch, *Nature* **392**, 51 (1998) [INSPEC].

7. G. Finkelstein, P. I. Glicofridis, R. C. Ashoori, M. Shayegan, *Science* **289**, 90 (2000) [INSPEC].

13. M. A. Eriksson, R. G. Beck, M. A. Topinka, J. A. Katine, R. M. Westervelt, K. L. Campman, A. C. Gossard, *Appl. Phys. Lett.* **69**, 671 (1996) [INSPEC].

14. R. Crook, C.G. Smith, M.Y. Simmons, D.A. Ritchie, *Phys. Rev. B* **62**, 5174 (2000) [INSPEC].

15. M. A. Topinka, B. J. LeRoy, S. E. J. Shaw, E. J. Heller, R. M. Westervelt, K. D. Maranowski, A. C. Gossard, *Nature* **410**, 183 (2001) [INSPEC].

16. M. A. Topinka, B. J. LeRoy, R. M. Westervelt, S. E. J. Shaw, R. Fleischmann, E. J. Heller, K. D. Maranowski, A. C. Gossard, *Nature* **410**, 183 (2001) [INSPEC].

17. B. J. van Wees, H. van Houten, C. W. J. Beenakker, J. G. Williamson, L. P. Kouwenhoven, D. van der Marel, C. T. Foxen, *Phy. Rev. Lett.* **60**, 848 (1988) [INSPEC]; D. A. Wharam, T. J.Thornton, R. Newbury, M. Pepper, H. Ahmed, J. E. F. Frost, D. G. Hasko, D. C. Peacock, D. A. Ritchie, G. A. C. Jones, *J. Phys. C* **21**, L209 (1988) [INSPEC].

Reprinted with permission from American Institute of Physics, © 2003
Authors: Mark A. Topinka, Robert M. Westervelt, and Eric J. Heller
Figure 4: Courtesy of the authors and originally printed in *Science*, 289 (2000)
Figure 5: Courtesy of the authors and originally printed in *Nature* 410 (2001)
Figure 6: Courtesy of S. E. J. Shaw, Harvard University, 2002

2

Applications of Electromagnetism and Electromagnetic Forces

On August 14, 2003, a blackout occurred that covered much of the northeastern United States and Canada. Although many people were quick to fault different political parties for this blackout, the fault may simply lie in the fact that our society is trying to use a vast, complex physical system in ways that lead to unpredictable behavior in that system.

The electric grid that supplies North America links every electrical source and consumer in Canada and the United States in a complicated network of transmission lines. The laws of physics govern this single machine, just like any other physical system. Power flows between two points in the system and along every path that connects to those points, meaning that any power exchanges affect the entire system. Each transmission line has a maximum capacity, and when arbitrary power exchanges occur, the power transmitted along each line becomes an unpredictable quantity. If the use of this system continues to be governed without serious *consideration of the physics controlling that system, author Eric Lerner predicts that more blackouts will occur. —LCK*

From "What's Wrong with the Electric Grid?"
by Eric J. Lerner
Industrial Physicist, October/November 2003

The warnings were certainly there. In 1998, former utility executive John Casazza predicted that "blackout risks will be increased" if plans for deregulating electric power went ahead. And the warnings continued to be heard from other energy experts and planners.

So it could not have been a great surprise to the electric-power industry when, on August 14, a blackout that covered much of the Northeast United States dramatically confirmed these warnings. Experts widely agree that such failures of the power-transmission system are a nearly unavoidable product of a collision between the physics of the system and the economic rules that now regulate it. To avoid future incidents, the nation must either physically transform the system to accommodate the new rules, or change the rules to better mesh with the power grid's physical behavior.

Understanding the grid's problems starts with its physical behavior. The vast system of electricity generation, transmission, and distribution that covers the United States and Canada is essentially a single machine—by many measures, the world's biggest machine. This single network is physically and

administratively subdivided into three "interconnects"—
the Eastern, covering the eastern two-thirds of the
United States and Canada; the Western, encompassing
most of the rest of the two countries; and the Electric
Reliability Council of Texas (ERCOT), covering most
of Texas. Within each interconnect, power flows through
AC lines, so all generators are tightly synchronized to
the same 60-Hz cycle. The interconnects are joined
to each other by DC links, so the coupling is much looser
among the interconnects than within them. (The
capacity of the transmission lines between the interconnects is also far less than the capacity of the links
within them.)

Prior to deregulation, which began in the 1990s,
regional and local electric utilities were regulated, vertical
monopolies. A single company controlled electricity
generation, transmission, and distribution in a given
geographical area. Each utility generally maintained
sufficient generation capacity to meet its customers'
needs, and long-distance energy shipments were usually
reserved for emergencies, such as unexpected generation
outages. In essence, the long-range connections served
as insurance against sudden loss of power. The main
exception was the net flows of power out of the large
hydropower generators in Quebec and Ontario.

This limited use of long-distance connections aided
system reliability, because the physical complexities of
power transmission rise rapidly as distance and the
complexity of interconnections grow. Power in an electric
network does not travel along a set path, as coal does,

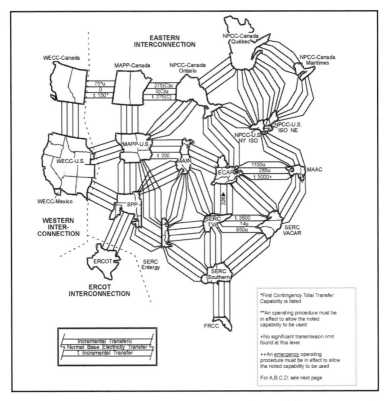

Figure 1: Normal U.S. base electricity transfers and first-contingency incremental transfer capabilities, in MW [megawatts]. *(North American Electric Reliability Council)*

for example. When utility A agrees to send electricity to utility B, utility A increases the amount of power generated while utility B decreases production or has an increased demand. The power then flows from the "source" (A) to the "sink" (B) along all the paths that can connect them. This means that changes in generation and transmission at any point in the system will change loads on generators and transmission lines at every other point—often in ways not anticipated or easily controlled.

To avoid system failures, the amount of power flowing over each transmission line must remain below the line's capacity. Exceeding capacity generates too much heat in a line, which can cause the line to sag or break or can create power-supply instability such as phase and voltage fluctuations. Capacity limits vary, depending on the length of the line and the transmission voltage. Longer lines have less capacity than shorter ones.

In addition, for an AC power grid to remain stable, the frequency and phase of all power generation units must remain synchronous within narrow limits. A generator that drops 2 Hz below 60 Hz will rapidly build up enough heat in its bearings to destroy itself. So circuit breakers trip a generator out of the system when the frequency varies too much. But much smaller frequency changes can indicate instability in the grid. In the Eastern Interconnect, a 30-mHz drop in frequency reduces power delivered by 1 GW.

If certain parts of the grid are carrying electricity at near capacity, a small shift of power flows can trip circuit breakers, which sends larger flows onto neighboring lines to start a chain-reaction failure. This happened on Nov. 10, 1965, when an incorrectly set circuit breaker tripped and set off a blackout that blanketed nearly the same area as the one in August.

After the 1965 blackout, the industry set up regional reliability councils, coordinated by the North American Electric Reliability Council, to set standards to improve planning and cooperation among the utilities. A single-contingency-loss standard was set up to keep the system functioning if a single unit, such as a generator or transition line, went out. Utilities built up spare generation and transmission capacity to maintain a safety margin. . .

. . . The new [1990s] regulations envisioned trading electricity like a commodity. Generating companies would sell their power for the best price they could get, and utilities would buy at the lowest price possible. For this concept to work, it was imperative to compel utilities that owned transmission lines to carry power from other companies' generators in the same way as they carried their own, even if the power went to a third party. FERC's Order 888 mandated the wheeling of electric power across utility lines in 1996. But that order remained in litigation until March 4, 2000, when the U.S. Supreme Court validated it and it went into force.

In the four years between the issuance of Order 888 and its full implementation, engineers began to warn that the new rules ignored the physics of the grid. The new policies "do not recognize the single-machine characteristics of the electric-power network," Casazza wrote in 1998. "The new rule balkanized control over the single machine," he explains. "It is like having every player in an orchestra use their own tunes."

In the view of Casazza and many other experts, the key error in the new rules was to view electricity as a commodity rather than as an essential service. Commodities can be shipped from point A through line B to point C, but power shifts affect the entire single machine system. As a result, increased long distance trading of electric power would create dangerous levels of congestion on transmission lines where controllers did not expect them and could not deal with them.

The problems would be compounded, engineers warned, as independent power producers added new generating units at essentially random locations determined by low labor costs, lax local regulations, or tax incentives. If generators were added far from the main consuming areas, the total quantity of power flows would rapidly increase, overloading transmission lines. "The system was never designed to handle long-distance wheeling," notes Loren Toole, a transmission-system analyst at Los Alamos National Laboratory.

At the same time, data needed to predict and react to system stress—such as basic information on the quantity of energy flows—began disappearing, treated by utilities as competitive information and kept secret. "Starting in 1998, the utilities stopped reporting on blackout statistics as well," says Ben Carreras of Oak Ridge National Laboratory, so system reliability could no longer be accurately assessed.

Finally, the separation into generation and transmission companies resulted in an inadequate amount of reactive power, which is current 90 deg out of phase with the voltage. Reactive power is needed to maintain voltage, and longer-distance transmission increases the need for it. However, only generating companies can produce reactive power, and with the new rules, they do not benefit from it. In fact, reactive-power production reduces the amount of deliverable power produced. So transmission companies, under the new rules, cannot require generating companies to produce enough reactive power to stabilize voltages and increase system stability.

The net result of the new rules was to more tightly couple the system physically and stress it closer to capacity, and at the same time, make control more diffuse and less coordinated—a prescription, engineers warned, for blackouts.

In March 2000, the warnings began to come true. Within a month of the Supreme Court decision implementing Order 888, electricity trading skyrocketed, as did stresses on the grid. One measure of stress is the number of transmission loading relief procedures (TLRs)—events that include relieving line loads by shifting power to other lines. In May 2000, TLRs on the Eastern Interconnect jumped to 6 times the level of May 1999. Equally important, the frequency stability of the grid rapidly deteriorated, with average hourly frequency deviations from 60 Hz leaping from 1.3 mHz in May 1999, to 4.9 mHz in May 2000, to 7.6 mHz by January 2001. As predicted, the new trading had the effect of overstressing and destabilizing the grid. . .

. . . The August 14 blackout, although set off by specific chance events, became the logical outcome of these trends. Controllers in Ohio, where the blackout started, were overextended, lacked vital data, and failed to act appropriately on outages that occurred more than an hour before the blackout. When energy shifted from one transmission line to another, overheating caused lines to sag into a tree. The snowballing cascade of shunted power that rippled across the Northeast in seconds would not have happened had the grid not been operating so near to its transmission capacity.

How to Fix It

The conditions that caused the August 14th blackout remain in place. In fact, the number of TLRs and the extent of frequency instability remained high after August 14 until September's cool weather reduced stress on the grid. What can be done to prevent a repetition next summer?

One widely supported answer is to change the grid physically to accommodate the new trading patterns, mainly by expanding transmission capacity. The DOE [Department of Energy] and FERC [Federal Energy Regulatory Commission], as well as organizations supported by the utilities, such as the Electric Power Research Institute and the Edison Electric Institute, advocate this approach. In reports before and after the blackout, they urged expanding transmission lines and easing environmental rules that limit their construction. The logic is simple: if increased energy trading causes congestion and, thus, unreliability, expand capacity so controllers can switch energy from line to line without overloading. . .

. . . But experts outside the utility industry point to serious drawbacks in the build-more solution other

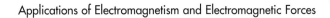

than increasing the cost of power. For one, it is almost impossible to say what level of capacity will accommodate the long-distance wholesale trading. The data needed to judge that is now proprietary and unavailable in detail. Even if made available to planners, this data refers only to the present. Transmission lines take years to build, but energy flows can expand rapidly to fill new capacity, as demonstrated by the jump in trading in the spring of 2000. New lines could be filled by new trades as fast as they go up.

The solution advocated by deregulation critics would revise the rules to put them back into accord with the grid physics. "The system is not outdated, it is just misused," says Casazza. "We should look hard at the new rules, see what is good for the system as a whole, and throw out the rest." Some changes could be made before next summer, and at no cost to ratepayers. For one thing, FERC or Congress could rescind Order 888 and reduce the long-distance energy flows that stress the system. Second, the data on energy flows and blackouts could again be made public so that planners would know what power flows are occurring and the reliability records of the utilities. Other changes, such as rehiring thousands of workers to upgrade maintenance, would take longer and might require rewriting regulations and undoing more of the 1992 Energy Act.

These changes also would have costs, but they would be borne by the shareholders and creditors of the banks and energy companies who bet so heavily on energy trading. With cash flows dwindling and debt levels high, many of these companies or their subsidiaries might face bankruptcy if energy trading is curtailed. The decision will ultimately fall to Congress, where hearings are scheduled for the fall. However the decision turns out, what is nearly certain is that until fixed, the disconnect between the grid's economics and physics will cause more blackouts in the future.

Capacitors are technically simple devices for storing electric energy. They are used in many different kinds of electronics, including computers, televisions, and audio amplifiers. However, in their standard forms, capacitors can store a somewhat small amount of energy, limiting their use to low energy consumption applications. Physicists Fritz Gassmann, Rüdiger Kötz, and Alexander Wokaun of the Paul Scherrer Institute, Switzerland, have taken up this challenge and created "supercapacitors," which exploit the large surface area of fractal geometry electrodes to expand the energy storage capacity of capacitors. The result of their research is a practical supercapacitor with enough energy storage capacity that it can power a car. This report on their efforts includes a brief review of basic capacitor physics and a succinct introduction to fractal geometry. —LCK

From "Supercapacitors Boost the Fuel Cell Car"

by Fritz Gassmann, Rüdiger Kötz, and Alexander Wokaun

Europhysics News, **September/October 2003**

No matter where you live it cannot have escaped your attention that our planet is struggling. There may be some who are sceptical but most of us can have little doubt that if we do not mend our ways, severe changes of global climate lie ahead. One of the most obvious major contributors to the deteriorating situation are the some 750 million registered vehicles worldwide that emit roughly 4 billion tons of carbon dioxide each year and contribute 15 % to the anthropogenic emissions. In addition to their impact on the global climate, several other facts are motivating car manufacturers to investigate ways of reducing emissions drastically: declining oil reserves, their location in politically unstable regions, and health hazards posed by secondary emissions of nitrogen oxides, hydrocarbons, and particulates. Today's most promising solution for these problems would be cars powered by fuel cells with solar hydrogen as the ultimate energy carrier. However, a number of obstacles are delaying widespread adoption of this technology including high costs, the weight and volume of today's fuel cells, security concerns related to hydrogen storage tanks, and the missing infrastructure needed for the production and distribution of hydrogen.

All these engineering and economic problems could be minimized if cars could be built without having excessive power, e.g. a 1 ton compact-class car with 20 kW continuous mechanical power at the wheel. Imagine such a car that could reach the maximum allowed speeds in most countries (120 km/h or 75 mph), climb over every pass (it would climb 6 % at a speed of 80 km/h or 50 mph) and transport people to their working places or shopping centres in the accustomed time (remember that powerful engines cannot help to lubricate a traffic jam). However, the hypothetical 20 kW car would need around 30 seconds to accelerate to 100 km/h (62 mph) and would, therefore, only be accepted by a few pioneers. The common technical answer of car manufacturers to this rather irrational but common human desire for power is oversizing engine power by a factor of about two to eight. The price customers pay for this solution is twofold: Powerful engines are more expensive, and, since these engines work below their optimum efficiency most of the time, their fuel consumption is high, causing increased operating costs and at the same time increased environmental damage.

Power Reserve for Fifteen Seconds

How do we escape from this trap? One solution is supercapacitors (also called supercaps, ultracapacitors, or electrochemical double layercapacitors, EDLC) which offer the possibility for electric cars to reconcile the widespread wish for power with environmental concerns.[1] Instead of designing the primary power system to deliver a maximum of e.g. 73 kW (100 horse-power), it could be designed for an average power of only 20 kW, with supercapacitors acting as power reserves to deliver peak power during a limited time. With 53 kW of additional power delivered over 15 seconds, most power display behaviour patterns could be satisfied: The car would accelerate to 100 km/h (62 mph) in less than 15 seconds, passing other cars over short distances would be possible, and enough rubber could be burned with starts to satisfy the speedster. Additional peak power of 53 kW over 15 seconds means access to an energy buffer of 220 Wh, an amount of energy costing a few cents when taken from the electric power grid.

Could the *lead-acid batteries* normally employed for the electric starter motors be used for this purpose? Two main limitations must be considered. Though a normal 12 V battery with a capacity of 60 Ah stores enough energy (720 Wh), the current should not exceed about 150 A, limiting the power to 1.8 kW, far below the desired 53 kW. Secondly, chemical reactions are taking place whenever current flows into or out of a battery. In principle the transformation from bulk lead sulfate into dissolved sulfate ions is completely reversible, but the decreasing mechanical stability of the lead sulfate electrode leads to degradation after several hundred charge/discharge cycles. In spite of considerable research on new battery concepts over the last decade, no battery has been found that would circumvent these limitations.

With *capacitors* used in practically all electronic devices, e.g. to smooth ripples on the DC current in power supply units, power and stability are no problem. As energy is stored by a purely physical process in

Physical relations for capacitors

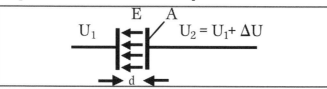

Both electrodes have a surface A (in m^2) separated by distance d (in m). The applied voltage ΔU (in Volt) creates an electrical field $E = \Delta U/d$ storing the electrical energy. Capacitance C in Farad (F) and stored energy J in Ws is:

$$C = \varepsilon_0 \cdot \varepsilon_r \frac{A}{d} \qquad J = \tfrac{1}{2} C \cdot \Delta U^2$$

where ε_r (e.g. 1 for vacuum or 81 for water) is the relative dielectric constant which depends on the material placed between the two electrodes and $\varepsilon_0 = 8.85 \cdot 10^{-12}$ F/m is a fundamental constant.

electric fields without involving chemical transformations, the number of loading cycles does not limit their lifetime. Furthermore, charge- or discharge-currents as measured in relation to the energy content, are about four decades higher than with batteries. The big disadvantage of traditional capacitors is their relatively small capacitance. This characteristic value (measured in *Farads*) relates to their energy content when multiplied by half the square of the applied voltage (see above, *Physical Relations for Capacitors*). A typical large electrolyte-capacitor used for power supplies has a capacitance of the order of 20'000 micro-Farad and allows a maximum voltage of about 20 V, storing only 4 Joules of energy, equivalent to 4 Ws or

0.0011 Wh. With a mass of about 20 g for such an element, roughly 4 tons would be needed to store the required energy of 220 Wh! . . .

Supercapacitors Combine Advantages of Battery and Capacitor

Over about the last decade, double-layer capacitors with unprecedented large capacitance have been developed in various research laboratories, and several companies have already started commercial production. At the Paul Scherrer Institute in Villigen, Switzerland, Rüdiger Kötz and his group have developed an electrode in collaboration with the Swiss company *montena* (recently merged with *Maxwell*). Towards the end of 2001, one of their supercapacitors reached a capacitance of 1600 Farad at a maximum voltage of 2.5 V. They store 5000 Joules or 1.4 Wh within a volume of roughly 0.3 L (5 cm diameter, 14 cm long) weighing 320 g. To store the required 220 Wh, 160 supercapacitors weighing 50 kg would suffice. With their small internal series resistance of 0.0014 Ohm, they can produce or absorb peak currents of over 300 A. Due to the excessively high currents at low voltages, operation is normally restricted to between 50 % and 100 % of maximum voltage and therefore, only 75 % of the energy capacity is used (due to the quadratic relationship between voltage and energy content, the residual energy equates to only 25 % at 50 % of the voltage). This restriction and also losses in power converters result in increasing the number needed from 160 to about 250 supercapacitors, weighing nearly 100 kg, including cables and electronics.

How to Build a Large Capacitor?

In a capacitor, energy is stored within the electric field between its electrodes in the following way: The application of a voltage between the electrodes results in the flow of electrons towards the negative electrode, and away from the positive electrode (see page 54: *Physical Relations for Capacitors*). This transport of electric charge towards and from the respective electrodes is equivalent to an electric current. Multiplication of this current by the applied voltage gives the power flowing into the electric field between the electrodes. The capacitance is determined by the geometric dimensions of the device and by the relative dielectric constant of the applied isolator foil. While this latter value lies between 1 for air to 81 for water and up to several 1000 for ceramics, more can be achieved by manipulating the geometry. Capacitance is proportional to the surface area of the electrodes divided by their separation distance, giving units of length (at the beginning of radio telecommunication, capacitors were therefore measured in cm). Simple capacitors consisting of two parallel plates reach only very small capacitances, of the order of pico-Farad ($1pF = 10^{-12}$ F), and are used in high frequency technology. Even when loaded to 1000 V, the energy content of such *plate capacitors* is only of the order of micro-Ws.

To increase the geometrical part of the capacitance, the surface area of the electrodes can be increased by rolling long stripes of conducting material, and at the same time, the isolating layer of material with high dielectric constant in between them is manufactured as thin as possible. With this technology, *rolled capacitors* of the order of 0.1 micro-Farad (1 μF = 10^{-6} F) resisting voltages up to about 1000 V can be produced, storing around 0.05 Ws of energy . . .

Another possible way to increase the geometrical part of the capacitance is to replace one of the electrodes by a liquid electrolyte (an electrically conducting gel) in order to achieve immediate geometrical contact on the atomic scale to the surface of a metallic electrode. A thin oxidic layer on the surface of the metal electrode serves as an isolator and separates the electrodes to distances of the order of nanometres, pushing capacitance into the tens of milli-Farad range (1 mF = 10^{-3} F) at maximum voltages of around 20–40 V. These so called *electrolyte capacitors* can store up to several Ws of energy . . .

Increasing the surface area by rolling and minimizing the separation distance to the molecular range long seemed the ultimate limit in the production of large capacitors. However, *fractal geometry* has opened amazing, and counterintuitive, new possibilities of how to scramble e.g. the surface of a football field into a 1 mm thick layer above a sheet of paper the size of the journal you are reading right now. By increasing the electrode surface about 100'000-fold in this way, electrolyte capacitors with thousands of Farad can be built.

The Mystery of the Inner Surface

Back at the beginning of the 20th century, "mathematical monsters" were invented: by an iterative process involving ever smaller lengths, linear objects with

Fractal Dimension

Assume a first measurement process performed with a stick of unit length. Obviously, it can be placed exactly once over the curve, and its finer structures are not detected. By repeating the measuring process with a measuring stick three times shorter than before (N=3), it can be placed four times (M=4) onto the "Koch curve." The same reasoning holds for any successive refinement of the measurement process. Consider now the well known definition $M=N^D$, holding for all smooth geometrical objects, giving D=0 (point), D=1 (line), D=2 (area), or D=3 (cube) when measured with successively smaller length scales. Applying the same definition for the "Koch curve" with N=3 and M=4 leads to a "fractal" dimension D= (log4)/(log3)≈1.2618. Over recent decades the concept of fractal dimension found numerous interesting applications in such diverse fields as geology, ecology, cosmology, physics and chemistry, medical sciences and economics.[2, 3] Step 0: Line of unit length is divided into 3 equal intervals. Step 1: The central interval is replaced by two lines of length 1/3, so increasing total length of the object by a factor of 4/3=1.3333. For the next step, the procedure is repeated for all four intervals, and so on. With an increasing number of iterations n, the length of the line gets therefore 1.3333^n and so exceeds every arbitrary large number, i.e. its length diverges towards infinity. A similar procedure leads to the well known Koch snowflake or Koch island.

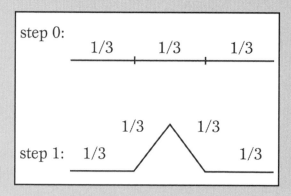

step 0:

1/3   1/3   1/3

1/3   1/3

step 1:   1/3   1/3

infinite length were created which could be fitted into a limited area, that was not at all filled up by the object. One of the most famous of these objects is the curve invented by the Swedish mathematician N. F. H. von Koch in 1906: A line of unit length is divided into three equal parts, the middle segment being replaced by two lines of length one third each. Obviously, repeated iteration leads to an ever longer path, because its length is multiplied by 4/3 with every iteration. On the other hand, the resulting line never exceeds a square of unit side length, nor does it need a considerable fraction of the square, because even a very long mathematical line still has zero surface. However, more and more points on the line are located close to an increasing number of points belonging to the surface of the square, yet eyeball inspection gives the impression that the geometrical object somehow combines the characteristics of a line and of a surface. With fractal dimension D, this qualitative property is put into an objective mathematical framework (see Box Two: *Fractal Dimension*).

Applying fractal geometry to increase the capacity,[4] the surface of the electrodes has been roughened by using soot particles in contact with the flat metallic carrier-foil of the electrode . . . A measurement of the fractal dimension of the borderline in a cross-section perpendicular to the electrode yields $D \approx 1.6$ . . . Using a general topological formula yields $D_S \approx 2.6$ for the overall dimension of the electrode surface. As self similarity of every physical object is limited to a maximum range between its macroscopic and the atomic scale, the concept of fractal dimension is also restricted to a limited range of length scales. Considering $D_s \approx 2.6$ as representative between the macroscopic scale of the electrode (of the order of 0.1 m) and the microscopic scale (in the order of 1 nm), self similarity can be assumed to hold over 8 decades. The electrode surface is therefore multiplied by 10 to the power of $8*(2.6-2)$ or 60'000. In combination with the extremely thin electrochemical double layer (around 1 nm), unprecedented capacitances can be reached. . .

References

1. R. Kötz and M. Carlen, *Principles and Applications of Electrochemical Capacitors*, Electrochimica Acta **45**, 2483–2498 (2000).
2. B. B. Mandelbrot, *Gaussian Self-Affinity and Fractals*, Springer, New York, Berlin, Heidelberg (2002).
3. H. M. Hastings and G. Sugihara, *Fractals—A User's Guide for Natural Sciences*, Oxford University Press (1993).
4. R. Richner, S. Müller, M. Bärtschi, R. Kötz and Wokaun, *Physically and Chemically Bonded Material for Double-Layer Capacitor Applications*, New Materials for Electrochemical Systems **5** (3), 297–304 (2002).

Reprinted with permission from *Europhysics* © 2003, Written by Fritz Gassman

Space exploration is exciting, capturing the imagination of humankind and promising access to resources and technological capabilities not available on Earth. But space exploration is also prohibitively expensive. Maintaining orbiting spacecraft in the usual way by bringing fuel up orbital heights could cost billions of dollars, for example. Motivated to reduce these costs and help make space exploration a reality, scientists

and engineers are investigating alternatives to standard energy sources in space. Dr. Enrico Lorenzini, who heads the Tethers in Space Research group at the Smithsonian Astrophysical Observatory, and professor Juan Sanmartín of the Polytechnic University of Madrid, are participants in those investigations and in this article tell of the promise of space tethers to produce artificial gravity, thrust, drag, and electric power for spacecraft.

To accomplish these tasks, space tethers use fundamental physics: the laws of forces on an orbiting body to create tension between the ends of the tether, and Faraday's law of charge motion in a magnetic field to generate an electric potential between those ends. The past thirty years have seen the science and engineering of these devices develop so much that space tethers are likely to become the indispensable workhorse of space exploration. —LCK

"Electrodynamic Tethers in Space"
by Enrico Lorenzini and Juan Sanmartín
Scientific American, August 2004

There are no filling stations in space. Every spacecraft on every mission has to carry all the energy sources required to get its job done, typically in the form of chemical propellants, photovoltaic arrays, or nuclear reactors.

The sole alternative—delivery service—can be formidably expensive. The International Space Station, for example, will need an estimated 77 metric tons of booster propellant over its anticipated 10-year life span just to keep itself from gradually falling out of orbit. Even assuming a minimal price of $7,000 a pound (dirt cheap by current standards) to get fuel up to the station's 360-kilometer altitude, that is $1.2 billion simply to maintain the orbital status quo. The problems are compounded for exploration of outer planets such as Jupiter, where distance from the sun makes photo-voltaic generation less effective and where every gram of fuel has to be transported hundreds of millions of kilometers.

So scientists are taking a new look at an experi-mentally tested technology—the space tether—that exploits some fundamental laws of physics to provide pointing, artificial gravity, electrical power, and thrust or drag, while reducing or eliminating the need for chemical-energy sources.

Tethers are systems in which a flexible cable connects two masses. When the cable is electrically conductive, the ensemble becomes an electrodynamic tether, or EDT. Unlike conventional arrangements, in which chemical or electrical thrusters exchange momentum between the spacecraft and propellant, and EDT exchanges momentum with the rotating planet through the mediation of the magnetic field. Tethers have long fascinated space enthusiasts. Visionaries such as Konstantin Tsiolkovsky and Arthur C. Clarke imagined using them as space elevators that whisked people from surface to orbit. In the mid-1960s two Gemini flights tested 30-meter tethers as a way to create artificial gravity from astronauts, and numerous kinds of tether experiments have taken place since then. The chief challenges are electromechanical: engineers have not yet devised reliable techniques to deal with the high voltages that EDTs experience in space. Nor have they solved all the issues of tether survivability in the hostile space environment or mastered the means to damp the types of vibrations to which EDTs are prone.

Nevertheless, many scientists believe that the technology could revolutionalize some types of spaceflight. Its applications cover low Earth orbit as well as planetary missions. EDTs are likely to find uses around Earth for cleaning up orbital debris and generating electricity at higher efficiency than fuel cells as well as keeping satellites in their desired orbits.

A Self-Adjusting System

Tethers exploit the sometimes counterintuitive quirks of orbital mechanics. Two countervailing forces act on any object in a stable orbit around a planet: an outward-pulling centrifugal force produced by orbital motion exactly balances a downward gravitational force. The gravity and centrifugal forces offset each other perfectly at the object's center of mass. An observer onboard is in zero g, or free fall, and does not perceive acceleration.

What happens if, instead of one compact satellite, we have two in slightly different orbits, connected by a tether? The tether causes the two satellites to act as a single system. The gravity and centrifugal forces still balance at the center of mass, halfway between the satellites, but they no longer balance at the satellites

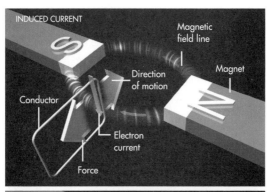

INDUCED CURRENT

Magnetic
field line

Magnet

Direction
of motion

Conductor

Electron
current

Force

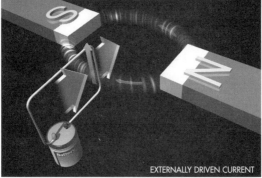

Battery

EXTERNALLY DRIVEN CURRENT

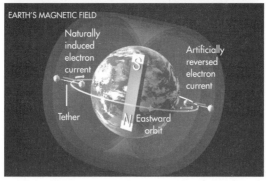

EARTH'S MAGNETIC FIELD

Naturally
induced
electron
current

Artificially
reversed
electron
current

Tether

Eastward
orbit

Electrodynamic tether systems have the potential to accomplish many of the same tasks as conventional spacecraft but without the need for large quantities of onboard fuel. They take advantage of two basic principles of electromagnetism: current is produced when conductors move through magnetic fields, and the field exerts a force on the current. Shown here are an induced current and an externally driven current. The third image shows how a current can control tether orbits.

themselves. At the outer satellite, the gravity force will be weaker and the centrifugal force stronger; a net force will thus push the satellite outward. The opposite situation occurs at the inner satellite, which is pulled inward.

What is happening is that the lower satellite, which orbits faster, tows its companion along like an orbital water-skier. The outer satellite thereby gains momentum at the expense of the lower one, causing its orbit to expand and that of the lower one to contract. As the satellites pull away from each other, they keep the tether taut. Nonconductive tethers are typically made of light, strong materials such as Kevlar (a carbon fiber) or Spectra (a high-strength polyethylene). Tensions are fairly low, typically from one half to five kilograms for nonrevolving tether systems.

The only equilibrium position of the system is with the tether aligned along the radial direction, called the local vertical. Every time the system tilts away from that configuration, a torque develops that pulls it back and makes it swing like a pendulum. This type of stabilization was used in the Earth-observing satellite GEOS-3 in 1975 to keep the satellite, equipped with a rigid boom several meters long, oriented toward Earth.

Researchers refer to the force imbalance between the two masses as the gravity gradient. Passengers would perceive it as mild gravity pulling them away from Earth on the outer satellite and toward Earth on the inner. In low Earth orbit (LEO, 200 to 2,000 kilometers), a 50-kilometer tether would provide about 0.01 g (1 percent of the gravity at Earth's surface). Astronauts would not be able to walk around: a person cannot get sufficient traction at less than 0.1 g. But for many purposes (tool use, showers, settling liquids), having a definitive "up" and "down" would obviously be superior to a completely weightless environment. And unlike other techniques for creating artificial gravity, this method does not require that the satellites revolve around each other.

An EDT, employing aluminum, copper, or another conductor in the tether cable, offers additional advantages. For one, it serves as an electrical generator: when a conductor moves through a magnetic field, charged particles in the conductor experience an electrodynamic force perpendicular to both the direction of motion and the magnetic field. So if a tether is moving from west to east through Earth's northward-pointing magnetic field, electrons will be induced to flow down the tether.

The tether exchanges electrons with the ionosphere, a region of the atmosphere in which high-energy solar radiation strips electrons from atoms, creating a jumble of electrons and ions, called a plasma. The tether collects free electrons at one end (the anode, or positively charged electron attractor) and ejects them at the opposite end (the cathode, or negatively charged electron emitter). The electrically conductive ionosphere serves to complete the circuit, and the result is a steady current that can be tapped to use for onboard power. As a practical matter, in LEO a 20-kilometer tether with a suitable anode design could produce up to 40 kilowatts of power, sufficient to run manned research facilities.

That capability has been recognized since the 1970s, when Mary Grossi of the Harvard-Smithsonian

Center for Astrophysics and Giuseppe Colombo of the University of Padua in Italy were the first to conduct research on EDTs. As many as 16 experimental missions have flown in space using either electrically conductive or nonconductive tethers.

In these early electrodynamic tether systems, a Teflon sleeve fully insulated the conductive part of the tether from the ionosphere, and the anode was either a large conductive sphere or an equivalent configuration to gather electrons. Such anodes, however, turned out to be relatively inefficient collectors. In the 1990s, for example, NASA and the Italian Space Agency jointly launched two versions of the 20-kilometer Tethered Satellite System (TSS). The TSS collected electrons using a metal sphere the size of a beach ball and convincingly demonstrated electrodynamic power generation in space. Despite those positive results, however, researchers discovered a difficulty that must be over-come before EDTs can be put to practical use. A negative net charge develops around a large spherical anode, impeding the flow of incoming electrons much as a single exit door creates a pileup of people when a crowd rushes to leave a single room.

One of us (Sanmartín) and his colleagues intro-duced the bare-tether concept to solve this problem. Left mostly uninsulated, the tether itself collects electrons over kilometers of its length rather than just at the tip. The tether benefits further from its thin, cylindrical geometry: electrons do not have to bunch up at one anode point, where their collective negative charge inhibits the arrival of more electrons. It need not be a round wire; a thin tape would collect the same current but would be much lighter.

A Nearly Free Lunch

All EDTs share an advantage: they can reduce or increase their velocity while in orbit by exploiting a fundamental principle of electromagnetism. A magnetic field exerts a force on a current-carrying wire according to the familiar "right-hand rule." Thus, for an EDT in eastward LEO, in which the electrons flow from top to bottom of the tether, the force is opposite to the direction of motion. The EDT experiences a resistance akin to air drag,which in turn lowers the tether system's orbit.

That may not seem like a desirable feature. But it is extremely attractive to planners concerned with sweeping up the large amount of space junk that now circles the planet in the form of dead satellites and spent upper stages of rockets. Indeed, the problem has been one of the motivations behind the development of tethers by NASA, universities, and small companies. At present, LEO is littered with several thousands of such objects, about 1,500 of which have a mass of more than 100 kilograms. Eventually atmospheric drag removes them from orbit by lowering their altitudes until they burn up on reentry into the dense lower atmosphere. Typically objects at an orbital altitude of 200 kilometers decay in several days, those at 400 kilometers in several months, and those at 1,000 kilometers in about 2,000 years.

If newly launched satellites carried EDTs that could be deployed at the end of their lifetimes, or if a robot manipulator could capture debris and carry it to an

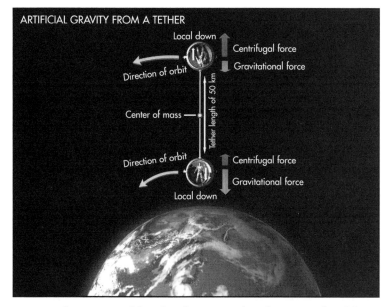

For any object in a stable orbit, the outward-pushing centrifugal force is exactly balanced by the inward-pulling gravitational force. In a tether system, all forces balance at the system's center of mass. But at the outer sphere, the centrifugal force is slightly larger than the gravitational force. As a result, a passenger would feel a slight "downward" force away from Earth—a form of artificial gravity (local down).

orbiting tether system, the drag effect could be used to speed up the reentry timetable. Conversely, reversing the direction of the current in an EDT in low Earth orbit (by using a photovoltaic array or other power supply) would produce the opposite effect. The tether system would experience a force in its direction of motion, yielding thrust instead of drag and raising its orbit. Propulsive EDTs could thus serve as space tugs to move payloads in LEO to a higher orbit or to counteract orbital decay. Recall the International Space Station's high-cost boost problem. If the ISS had employed an electrodynamic tether drawing 10 percent of the station's power, it would need only 17 tons of propellant (as opposed to 77 in the current design) to avoid orbital decay; more power would nearly eliminate the need for propellant. Also, switching on a propulsive EDT at the right time along the orbit can produce lateral forces useful for changing the inclination of any spacecraft in orbit—an operation that requires a large amount of fuel when it is carried out with chemical thrusters.

Of course, conservation of energy demands that there is no "free lunch." For instance, power is generated only at the expense of the satellite's altitude, which was originally achieved by expending energy in rocket engines. So it may seem at first glance as if EDTs merely exchange one kind of energy for another in a rather pointless exercise. In drawing power from the tether, the satellite would descend and require reboosting. A fuel cell, in contrast, converts fuel into electricity directly. So why bother?

The answer is that the tether system is potentially more efficient, however paradoxical it may appear. The combination tether/rocket can generate more electrical power than a fuel cell can because the cell does not profit from the orbital energy of its fuel, whereas the tether/ rocket does. In an EDT, the electrical power produced is the rate of work done by the magnetic drag—that is, the magnitude of the drag force times the velocity of the satellite (relative to the magnetized ionosphere), which is about 7.5 kilometers per second in LEO. By comparison, the chemical power generated by a rocket equals one half the thrust times the exhaust velocity. A mixture of liquid hydrogen and liquid oxygen produces an exhaust with a speed as high as five kilometers per second. In practical terms, therefore, a tether/rocket combination could generate three times as much electrical power as the chemical reaction alone produces. A fuel cell, which also uses hydrogen and oxygen, has no such advantage.

The combination tether/rocket might consume substantially less fuel than a fuel cell producing equal power. The tradeoff is that the tether is heavier than the fuel cell. Thus, use of a tether to generate power will result in overall savings only for a period longer than five to ten days.

Tethers, by Jove

In certain circumstances, such as a mission to explore Jupiter and its moons, tether systems have further advantages. By exploiting the giant planet's physical peculiarities, a tether system could eliminate the need for enormous amounts of fuel. Like Earth, Jupiter has a magnetized ionosphere that rotates with the planet. Unlike Earth, its ionosphere persists beyond the stationary orbit—the altitude at which a given object remains above the same location on the planet's surface. For Earth, that is about 35,800 kilometers; for Jupiter, about 88,500 kilometers about the cloud tops.

In a Jovian stationary orbit, a spacecraft goes around the planet at the same speed as the ionosphere. So if the spacecraft descends below stationary altitude, where the speed of the magnetized plasma is lower than the speed of the spacecraft, the natural output of an EDT is a drag force, along with usable electrical power from the tether current. Alternatively, above the stationary orbit, where the magnetized plasma moves faster than the spacecraft, the natural result is thrust and usable electrical power.

Again, this might appear to be a free-lunch scenario. But it is not. The energy is taken from the planet's rotation in both cases. Jupiter's collective momentum, however, is so vast that the tiny amount expended on the spacecraft is negligible.

According to the principles of orbital dynamics, the most efficient places to apply drag or thrust are the points in the orbit nearest (periapsis) and farthest (apoapsis) from Jupiter. The natural force will be drag if the point lies inside the stationary orbit and thrust if it lies outside. Assume that a tether-bearing spacecraft would approach Jupiter with a relative velocity of about six kilometers per second. If drag were not applied, the spacecraft would fly past Jupiter. But if the tether were turned on as the spacecraft came inside the stationary orbit, it could brake the motion just enough to put the spacecraft in an elongated, highly eccentric ellipse around Jupiter. Capture into such an orbit requires reducing the velocity by only hundreds of meters per second. A tether tens of kilometers long would suffice.

As the spacecraft went around and around Jupiter, mission controllers would turn on the tether near periapsis to produce drag (and usable power) and turn it off elsewhere. That gradually would reduce the orbit from an elongated ellipse to smaller, progressively more circular shapes. The spacecraft would then require only modest electrodynamic forces to visit each of the four largest moons of Jupiter from the outermost (Callisto) to the innermost (Io). With Callisto's orbital period of about half a month, the entire sequence could take less than a year.

To return, controllers would reverse the process. They would first switch on the EDT at apoapsis, which lies outside the stationary orbit, to produce thrust and power. The repeated thrust applications at apoapsis would raise periapsis from inside to outside the stationary orbit. Now thrust could be generated (for "free" again) at periapsis, progressively increasing the altitude of apospsis. A final push could boost the spacecraft out of orbit for transfer back to Earth. Tapping Jupiter's rotation would provide all the energy for these maneuvers as well as generate usable power. By reducing drastically the fuel and power requirements, the tether would greatly cut the cost of a mission.

The technology of space tethers has matured tremendously in the past 30 years. But it still faces several challenges before EDTs can be put to practical use in orbit around Earth, Jupiter, or elsewhere. Designers will have to devise ways to protect tethers from the effects of high electrical potential between the tether and the ionosphere as well as from the slow degradation of materials in space. And they must learn to control the various vibrations that arise in electro-dynamic tether systems. These obstacles are not insuperable, however, and many scientists expect to see tethers doing real work in the not so distant future.

3

Electromagnetic Forces Applied in Scientific Research

Electromagnetic forces have proven useful for countless applications since scientists and engineers began to study such forces in the 1800s. New ways to use electromagnetic forces are still being explored, leading to exciting possibilities for further technological advancement. Stuart A. Solin, a professor of experimental physics at the College of Arts and Sciences at Washington University, tells the story of discovery of "extraordinary magnetoresistance," called EMR, in semiconductor "superlattices." EMR is an effect caused by the force felt by electrons traveling in a magnetic field. When a magnetic field is applied to an EMR device, the electrons are forced to travel at an angle to the electric field lines, which they would normally follow. When the electrons are flowing through or near metal disks inserted inside the semiconductor, the magnetic field can change the disk from acting as a very low resistance path to a very high resistance path for the electrons. In this way, the magnetic field switches the resistance of the material from very low to very high. With this new capability for controlling a material property of semiconductors, a new field for development of fast computer disk drives, automotive control systems, and other applications is made possible. —LCK

"Magnetic Field Nanosensors"
by Stuart A. Solin
Scientific American, July 2004

It often happens in science that research focused on one phenomenon results in the unexpected discovery of a new effect that is much more exciting and important. In 1995 a case of this serendipity occurred with my research group, then at the NEC research Institute in Princeton, N.J.

We were studying the properties of a microelectronics structure called a semiconductor superlattice, which consisted of layers of gallium arsenide and gallium aluminum arsenide stacked like a club sandwich. We knew that this superlattice had very interesting electrical properties. In particular, we were investigating how the thickness of the layers determined whether the super-lattice behaved as a metal, with low electrical resistance, or as an insulator, with high resistance. We immersed the system in a magnetic field, a procedure that enabled us to study dynamical processes involving the electrons in the superlattice.

To our great surprise, we saw that the resistance of the superlattice increased dramatically when we strengthened the magnetic field. Such behavior would be expected in a magnetic material but not in something like our superlattice, which was made entirely of non-magnetic constituents. The percentage increase in resistance, called the magnetoresistance (MR), was so big and so unusual that my team immediately redirected its efforts to explain the fundamental physics of this new effect.

By 1997 we had developed a sound basic understanding of this new kind of large MR. Moreover, we predicted that considerably greater MR might be obtained from a much simpler structure fabricated from a nonmagnetic metal such as gold (Au) and a single layer of the semiconductor indium antimonide (InSb). In 1998, working with Jean Heremans of Ohio University, we built an InSb-Au structure that fulfilled our prediction. In a magnetic field of five teslas, the MR was about 1 million percent at room temperature, thousands of times as great as any MR previously observed at that temperature. We dubbed this phenomenon "extraordinary magnetoresistance," or EMR, and we knew that it could be useful for a wide variety of technologies that require sophisticated magnetic field sensors, such as ultrahigh-density data recording, automotive control systems, industrial applications, medical devices, and consumer electronics.

What's So Special About EMR

EMR was far from being the first large MR effect discovered. In recent decades, a series of such phenomena have been observed, in part as a response to the demand for small yet highly sensitive magnetic field sensors. EMR is unique among large MRs, however, in that it does not require a magnetic material as part of the structure—a property that is scientifically intriguing and also advantageous for certain applications, as I will explain later.

The other big MR effects occur when the magnetic field of a material's atoms interacts with the intrinsic magnetism of the electrons flowing through the material. You can picture the innate magnetism of the electrons by imagining that each one contains a tiny bar magnet with a north and a south pole. Normally these magnets point in random directions and have no effect on the flow of current. But in a magnetic material, the electrons tend to become polarized, with their magnets aligned with the material's magnetic field. Once an electric current is polarized, it flows more easily through a material whose magnetic field is parallel with its polarization than through one that is antiparallel.

Thus, MR structures typically have one layer of magnetic material that polarizes the current and a second layer that has a controllable magnetization; the second layer impedes or lets through the current depending on how its field is oriented with respect to the first layer. Devices that utilize the electron's magnetism in this way are called either magnetoelectronics or spintronics, the latter because the magnetism is closely related to a quantity called spin.

How, then, does EMR work in the absence of a magnetic material? The answer lies in a second way that magnetic fields interact with moving electrons.

When a charged particle, such as an electron, travels through a magnetic field, the field exerts a transverse force on the particle, curving its trajectory. This effect is what causes ordinary MR. The field curves the electrons' trajectories, even turning them into helices if it is strong enough. Because the electrons travel along longer, winding paths, their net motion from one end of the material to the other is slowed down. In this way, the current is reduced; the resistance is enhanced. To be more precise, the electrons actually travel along random zigzag paths because of collisions with impurities or other defects in the material. Nevertheless, the magnetic field turns each straight zig or zag into a curve, increasing the total path length traveled as the electrons make their erratic way through the material.

The very much larger effect of EMR also depends on the magnetic field curving the electrons' paths. EMR's great magnitude, however, is caused by the interplay of the curved paths and the detailed geometry of the EMR device at the nanometer scale (billionths of a meter). The shape, location, and electrical properties of the elements of the device—such as electrical contacts and regions of different materials—can all contribute to this geometrically based MR.

For magnetic MR devices and ordinary MR in nonmagnetic semiconductors, the geometric contribution to the MR is insignificant compared with the physical contribution (the part that depends on the intrinsic physical properties of the material, such as the number of electrons per unit volume available to carry a current).

By designing novel hybrid structures of nonmagnetic semiconductors and metals, my group was able to construct devices in which the geometric contribution to the MR far exceeded the physical contribution.

Understanding EMR

To understand EMR, consider the device shown at the bottom of the illustration on page 80. The key part is a disk of gold that is embedded in a thin slab of narrow-gap semiconductor, such as InSb. (The "gap" of a semiconductor is a band of quantum states forbidden to its electrons, the size of which influences many of the material's electronic properties.) The conductivity of the metal is about 2,000 times greater than that of the semiconductor.

When we apply a voltage across electrical contacts at each end of the slab, current flows through the device. The current flows along electric field lines that the voltage establishes in the material. A property of electric field lines is that they tend to align themselves at right angles to the outside surface of a good conductor. This effect causes them to curve inward and concentrate on the metal disk. The current is thus funneled through the highly conductive metal, which causes the device as a whole to have a low resistance. The exact value of the resistance will depend on the geometry—that is, on the relative dimensions and shape of the metal and semiconductor.

Now consider what happens if we apply a magnetic field perpendicular to the slab. As in ordinary MR, the field produces an additional force on the charges,

PRODUCING THE EXTRAORDINARY

Magnetoresistance arises when a magnetic field changes the configuration of electric fields in a piece of semiconductor, reducing the current flow. "Extraordinary" magnetoresistance (EMR) occurs when the geometry of a metal-semiconductor device interacts with the electric fields to greatly accentuate the effect.

CURRENT FLOW IN A SEMICONDUCTOR

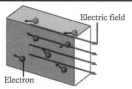

When a voltage is applied across the ends of a slab of semiconductor, it sets up an electric field that causes randomly moving electrons to drift along the slab on average.

That drift of electrons adds up to an electric current flowing in parallel to the electric field lines. By convention, the direction of current flow is opposite to that of the electron drift.

A MAGNETIC CROSSWIND

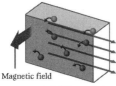

When a magnetic field is applied transversely, it curves the electrons' trajectories. That effect increases the path length that the electrons travel, which reduces their average drift velocity along the slab. Thus, the current is reduced, producing magnetoresistance.

The curved paths also cause electrons to accumulate on the bottom surface of the slab and holes (positively charged absences of electrons) to accumulate on top. Together those charges generate a transverse electric field. The current flow is at an angle to the total electric field, deflected by the magnetic field.

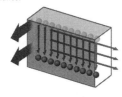

When the magnetic field is strong enough, the transverse electric field overwhelms the original electric field. Current now flows at a right angle to the electric field lines.

EXTRAORDINARY MAGNETORESISTANCE

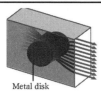

A metal disk implanted in the semiconductor distorts the electric field lines, which are approximately perpendicular to a conductor's outer surface. The field lines and the current flow are concentrated through the metal disk, so more current flows through the device than when the disk is absent. That is, the device resistance is very low.

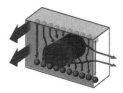

When a strong magnetic field is applied, again charges build up at top and bottom, the vertical electric field overwhelms the original field, and the electric field is distorted to be perpendicular to the metal disk. Again the current flow is at right angles to the electric field lines, which now causes the current to skirt around the disk. Being squeezed through narrow strips of semiconductor drastically reduces the current; the device's resistance is greatly increased—extraordinary magnetoresistance.

deflecting them like a plane in a crosswind, so that they travel at an angle to the electric field lines. Given a strong enough magnetic field, they can be deflected a full 90 degrees at the boundary of the metal disk. In other words, the current flows around the perimeter of the metal disk instead of entering it. (There is a little more to the story than that, as is explained in the illustration, but the current's avoiding of the metal disk is the key end result.)

The current behaves exactly as if the metal disk was replaced by a big cavity in the semiconductor that had to be circumnavigated. Such a structure—a semiconductor with a disk cut out of it, which squeezes the current through the two narrow channels of semiconductor— has a much higher resistance than an uninterrupted slab of semiconductor (which itself has higher resistance than a semiconductor with a disk of metal embedded in it). Thus, at zero magnetic field the metal disk acts as a short circuit (very low resistance), and in a strong enough field it is equivalent to an empty space—an open circuit (very high resistance). This change in state produces the EMR effect.

Achieving this understanding of EMR was greatly stimulated by the pioneering work of Charles Wolf and Lester Stillman of the University of Illinois, who in the 1970s studied structures made of semiconductor and metal (called hybrid structures). In particular, they looked at the hybrid structures' carrier mobility, which is a measure of the ease with which the carriers of electric current move in an electric field. Carriers can be electrons or holes. A hole is the absence of an electron from a sea of electrons that behaves in many ways like a positively charged particle.

Building on Wolf and Stillman's work, my colleagues and I realized that the EMR in weak magnetic fields ought to be much bigger for semiconductors with higher carrier mobility. Narrow-gap materials such as InSb have the requisite high mobility. This prediction prompted efforts to develop semiconductor materials with increased mobility. Lesley Cohen and the late Tony Stradling of Imperial College London made significant progress preparing high-mobility, ultrathin films of InSb. Michael Santos of the University of Oklahoma has successfully focused on heterostructures (structures combining two types of semiconductor) made of InSb and indium aluminum antimonide (InAlSb) layers. Dirk Grundler and his colleagues at Hamburg University in Germany have carried out extensive studies of EMR in indium arsenidemetal hybrid structures.

Myriad Applications

Two factors have driven the discovery and study of MR phenomena during the past 16 years: pure intellectual curiosity and the promise of technological applications for magnetic sensors. That promise has certainly been realized in the case of giant MR, or GMR, which was discovered in 1988. Most, if not all, of the magnetic disk drives used in today's computers employ GMR read-head sensors to detect the magnetic bits of stored information.

MR sensors in general and EMR sensors in particular have myriad potential applications. Industrial ones include process monitors, position-sensing robots for factory production lines, magnetic-field testing for machinery and engines, speed sensing for gears, and position sensors for ferromagnetic parts. Some automotive applications are antilock brakes, "smart" shock absorbers, vehicle counting systems, and ignition timing and control systems. Consumers benefit from the sensors in flip-phone switches, solid-state compasses, nonvolatile memory in low-cost appliances, elevator control switches, and noiseless motor controls in disk drives. They might see the gadgets used in banks to do currency sorting and counting based on magnetic inks. Sensors of both low and high fields could also find uses in medical devices.

Of these applications, computer disk drive read heads are probably the most technologically challenging. Disk drives have three key components: the magnetic disk medium, which stores the information, the write head element, which writes information onto the disk, and the read-head element, which reads the information. All three components will have to be improved significantly to satiate the ongoing demand for low-cost, high-speed storage at ever-greater densities.

A bit of information on a magnetic disk consists of a small magnetized region that produces a minute magnetic field just above that spot on the disk. For simplicity, you can think of a field pointing up out of the disk as a "one" and a field pointing down into the disk as a "zero." Every square inch of a modern disk drive has about 20 billion of these bits, for a density of

20 gigabits per square inch (Gb/in^2). As the size of the bit is reduced to increase storage density, the read head must be shrunk and its sensitivity must increase to detect the weaker magnetic field of the smaller bit. The head must also respond to the field faster, because a smaller bit on the rotating disk spends less time under it.

In evaluating a read head, what really matters is not the raw magnitude of the MR effect but the head's signal-to-noise ratio, which depends on a number of other factors in addition to the amount of MR. A major source of noise for all MR sensors that use magnetized materials—that is, all but EMR—is magnetic noise. This effect occurs because the magnetism in the material is generated by innumerable magnetic atoms, like a host of tiny bar magnets, all roughly aligned but randomly fluctuating like compass needles being jiggled about. For large volumes of material, the fluctuations average out to be negligible relative to the total magnetism. As the sensor volume decreases, however, the proportion of noise increases. Magnetic noise might fundamentally limit read heads based on magnetic materials to data densities of a few hundred Gb/in^2, yet the five-year target for the magnetic recording industry is 1,000 Gb/in^2, or one terabit per square inch (Tb/in^2). Because read heads based on EMR use nonmagnetic materials, they would not suffer from magnetic noise limitations. They thus represent a possible option for the design of a 1-Tb/in^2 read head.

But a density of 1 Tb/in^2 corresponds to each bit occupying a square 25 nanometers on a side. The read

head needs to be of similar size. Fabricating a viable, nanoscopic EMR device is a significant scientific and technological challenge. The scientific problem is to design a nanoscopic device with sufficient EMR to be of practical use. When one crosses into the nanoscopic regime, the physics of the electrical conduction process changes in a way that significantly reduces EMR. Technologically, one must design a workable EMR nanostructure that can be fabricated using convenient techniques. Unfortunately, the disk structures used in the first demonstration of EMR are not easily scalable to nanoscopic dimensions. To meet these challenges, the NEC Princeton team was expanded to include physicists J. Shen Tsai and Yu. A. Pashkin of NEC Japan, who are, respectively, experts in the electrical conduction of nanostructures and in the methods of electron-beam lithography used to fabricate them.

The basic EMR device that I described earlier is said to be internally shunted—the metal disk (the shunt) lies inside a ring of semiconductor, like an island surrounded by a circular moat. My expanded NEC team realized that this geometry could be rearranged by a mathematical process called conformal mapping to form an externally shunted device. The end result is that the semiconductor and the metal form two strips side by side, with all the electrical contacts—two for sensing voltage, two for passing a current in and out—along the free edge of the semiconductor. The shunt (a strip of conductive metal) is now on the outside, across from the electrical contracts. It is not easy to describe in words what shape the electric field lines take or how the flowing carriers get deflected from those lines by a magnetic field (and hence avoid the conducting metal). But the magic of a conformal mapping is that the device is guaranteed to operate in identical fashion to the circular version, just with the geometry of all the critical elements (semiconductor, metal, field lines, and current flows) transformed by the mapping. The linear, external-shunt version has the added advantage that it can be readily constructed and operated at nanoscopic sizes.

To make our devices, we used state-of-the-art electron-beam lithography—and airplanes: our samples traveled back and forth between Princeton to Tsukauba four times during their fabrication. The final result was worth all the miles that were clocked. We ended up with EMR devices—made from the Santos type of heterostructures—that had raw data density of about 700 GB/in^2. The practicalities of incorporating this proof-of-principle device into a working read head will probably roughly halve that density. To date, our group's design has achieved MR values in excess of 35 percent at a field of 0.05 tesla—good enough, I believe, for practical technology.

A Puzzle

While striving to grasp the fundamental physics of the EMR effect in the nanoscopic-size regime, we realized that the device we had fabricated *should not work*. It "should" have an EMR of less than 1 percent. The reason has to do with how the electrons (or holes) travel in random zigzag paths that drift in the direction of the current flow (called diffusive transport). The average length of each straight section (the distance traveled between collisions with defects) is called the mean free path. Some of the elements of our nanoscopic structure are smaller than the mean free path. Consequently, a charge carrier is much more likely to strike the sidewall of the structure before it has a chance to ricochet from a defect. Therefore, a carrier's motion through the device is ballistic—it transverses the device in a straight line, not by zigzags. It works out that a magnetic field deflects ballistic carriers that are confined in nanoscopic structures much less than it does diffusive carriers traversing macroscopic structures. Thus, the smaller deflection at the metal-semiconductor interface in a nanoscopic device significantly reduces the EMR.

Fortunately, and not by design, our fabrication process produced rippled sidewalls with an approximate periodicity that enhanced the scattering of carriers striking them. This scattering transformed the carrier motion from ballistic to diffusive, and the large EMR associated with diffusive transport resulted. Serendipity, which led to the original discovery of the EMR phenomenon, was repeated in the process of fabricating a viable nanoscopic prototype! Happily, we now know why these ripples form, and we believe that we can control their size.

EMR read heads would have many good features in addition to the high data densities and low magnetic noise. Their intrinsic response speed could be more than 100 times as fast as that of other read heads. They can be integrated onto semiconductor substrates easily and should have low fabrication costs. A disadvantage is the need to operate at relatively low temperatures— not much warmer than room temperature. One feature is both an advantage and a disadvantage: the response of the EMR read heads increases with the square of the magnetic field strength. That behavior is "nonlinear" (which is bad) but makes for high sensitivity (which is good).

The biggest challenge to present is that EMR sensors are still a new and unproved technology. Significant technological and economic barriers must be overcome if EMR is to be commercially successful for magnetic recording. Such obstacles are not atypical in the development of potentially disruptive technologies. Indeed, other disruptive technologies could render an EMR read head obsolete before it is even developed. Heat-assisted magnetic recording (HAMR), which is being worked on at Seagate Corporation, and Millipede non-magnetic recording, an IBM project, are examples of competing technologies. Yet even if that happens, EMR's discoverers hope to see EMR employed for a number of the other applications I have cited. What lies ahead is the hard work necessary to bring serendipity's two generous gifts to fruition.

When I press my fingers together, I can feel the force of one pressing against the other. This force must be the electromagnetic force, the clouds of electrons circling the atoms in one finger repelling the clouds of electrons circling the atoms in the other finger. It is the same when any two objects press against each other. When those two objects are atomic in scale, the forces take on their quantum identities. Chemical bonds may form between the two objects, where the electrons in one object become indistinguishable from the electrons in the second object. Quantum mechanical "tunneling" of electrons can occur, where an electron can jump through the potential barrier separating the two objects. These and other effects are used in scanning probe microscopes (SPMs), which image molecules and atoms or measure material properties.

The collection of force-based microscopes briefly discussed in this article includes the atomic force microscope (AFM), the friction force microscope (FFM), and the magnetic force microscope (MFM). By dragging tiny tips across nanometer-sized features in material surfaces, these microscopes uncover a world we could otherwise only imagine. This is a world scientists and engineers need to image as they develop new technologies, such as magnetic data storage media. Micro- and nanotechnology expert Ineke Malsch has found that the tiny tips that probe this nanoworld are essential tools for the job. —LCK

From "Tiny Tips Probe Nanotechnology"
by Ineke Malsch
The Industrial Physicist, October/November 2002

Industry wants precise nanoscale measurements and materials characterization for the production and quality control of nanostructures. Attaining these measurements, however, has proved more difficult than designing and fabricating such structures. In recent years, advances in scanning probe microscopes (SPMs) have led some companies to install these devices in-line for repeatable, accurate measurements of structures in three dimensions.

Since the 1980s, researchers and companies have developed several SPM types and subtypes to image and manipulate nanostructures, including atoms and molecules. Scanning tunneling microscopes (STMs) can image the atomic structure of conducting crystalline surfaces. Scanning near-field optical microscopes (SNOMs) can create optical images of delicate structures—for example, biological molecules on surfaces. Atomic force microscopes (AFMs) can image and analyze a surface down to atomic resolution regardless of its electrical conductivity. Although these instruments are still mostly applied in research and product development, the semiconductor and several other industries are beginning to use AFMs in quality control.

SPMs use a sharp tip, the probe, which touches or nearly touches a sample's surface to create images or measure the properties of materials. The AFM, in particular, provides two major advantages over optical and scanning electron microscopes—nanometer resolution and three-dimensional images. Manual SPMs usually consist of four elements:

- a piezoelectric or flexure-stage scanner, which scans the sample surface with the probe;
- a detector to read the probe–sample interaction;
- a control station, which includes a computer and an SPM controller–electronics unit that controls the SPM's operation and generates and analyzes digital images; and
- a stage, the structure on which the probe, scanner, and accessories rest during imaging.

In many models, the scanner and detector are combined into one unit, usually called the SPM head.

In general, industry relies more on manual than automated SPMs, but automated units have become almost indispensable in the semiconductor and data-storage industries. Various levels of automation are available, including for the measurement of batch-produced samples, analysis of several images at once, and, at the high end, the interfacing of the microscope with other hardware to minimize human handling of semiconductor wafers during fabrication and to make hundreds of identical measurements in real time.

Origins

Heinrich Rohrer and Gerd Binnig of IBM's Zurich
Research Laboratory received the 1987 Nobel Prize in
Physics for inventing the STM, the first of the SPMs, in
1981. The STM functions by scanning a tip along a
conducting surface and measuring the tunneling current
between surface and tip. The result is an image of the
electron cloud of the surface atoms. STMs can provide
subatomic resolution in lateral and vertical directions.
The STM allows the study of atomic structures on
conducting or semiconducting surfaces, and it is widely
used to study layer growth in the semiconductor industry.

The SNOM functions by tunneling light through a
small hole, which enables the measurement of structures
that are smaller than the wavelength of the light itself.
D. W. Pohl, now at the University of Basel in Switzerland,
and colleagues invented the SNOM in 1984. Even very
small structures on a surface, such as a biological molecule, reflect light in the visible spectrum. However,
biological molecules are smaller than the wavelengths
of the light used in optical microscopes. Hence, the
contribution of a single molecule is too small for a
normal optical microscope to distinguish.

In a SNOM, the probe consists of an optical fiber
with a sharp tip covered with a nonoptical coating that
has a small opening at the end. The tip is brought in
contact with the sample and moved across it to illuminate
the surface. The light does not directly image the sample,
but as the tip moves, a tiny dithering motion occurs in
the X–Y plane. The microscope relies on this contact

and motion to generate the topographical image. The advantage of the SNOM is that it generates an optical image alongside a topographical image. SNOMs are used to study living cells and biomolecules; for characterization and analysis applications in optoelectronics and telecommunication; and in imaging structures on transparent surfaces.

Atomic Forces

Gerd Binnig and Christoph Gerber of IBM Zurich and Cal Quate of Stanford University invented the AFM in 1986. This instrument measures atomic forces on a surface by scanning a sharp tip attached to a flexible cantilever across the sample. The tip diameter can be as small as 5 nm (10^{-9} m). An optical readout or a piezoelectric crystal translates the motion of the cantilever into an electronic signal. The outcome is a three-dimensional image of the surface structure displayed on a screen. Maximum resolution is typically on the atomic scale in the lateral and vertical dimensions, and the AFM enables the measurement of forces as small as 10^{-12} N. "This allows atomic resolution and interacting with the short-range forces of the chemical bonds," Gerber says. "With these characteristics, the instrument has surpassed the resolution of the STM on distinct surfaces."

Over the years, researchers have adapted the AFM and its functioning to suit different applications. In the contact mode, the cantilever lightly drags the tip across the surface and follows the surface structure. Contact is necessary for applications such as scratch tests. In the tapping or noncontact mode, the AFM cantilever–tip assembly oscillates up and down as it scans across the surface. This mode is much less disruptive to soft samples such as delicate biological molecules or certain surface features.

AFM tips play a key role in performance. Their useful lifetime varies with the type of sample, its topography, and the imaging mode. Some tips operating on automated systems will endure for days without breaking, while others may last for only a few uses. Tips are usually made of silicon or silicon nitride, and they may be uncoated or coated with materials such as aluminum, a cobalt alloy, or diamond, depending on their intended use. Sometimes, tiny spheres are used instead of tips, not for imaging but for various force measurements.

Researchers continue to adapt the AFM to measure other properties, including chemical, mechanical, electrical, and magnetic. The friction force microscope (FFM) moves a sharp tip across a surface in the contact mode. The friction between the surface and tip twists the cantilever. A laser beam, reflected by the cantilever, hits an optical detector screen. The location of the detected light is a measure of the cantilever's torsion and, hence, of friction. Thus, FFMs can acquire chemical contrast images, which show different chemical compositions of distinct surface areas and have many applications, including in polymer blends, polymer wetting, and thin-film technology.

FFMs allow the study of the basic mechanisms of sliding under various environmental conditions. "The company IAVF in Karlsruhe, Germany, investigates surfaces of machine parts, applying FFM," says Ernst

Meyer of the Institute of Physics at the University of Basel. "They characterize the tribomutated layer that forms after the running in of a machine. This layer is only 10 to 50 nm thick, but it determines the long-term performance of the motor." Other companies use FFMs in research on friction and rheology between two machine parts. "In our own institution, we have proved that one monolayer of lubricant is enough to reduce friction by a factor of 10," Meyer says.

The magnetic force microscope (MFM) is a non-contact AFM. It can measure the stray field of ferromagnetic and superconducting samples, which indicates the location of ferromagnetic domain walls. And it can locate vortices in superconductors, which result from surface defects. The MFM tip also can change the magnetic state of a sample. Widely used for quality control in the data-storage industry, it can determine the sensitivity and response of magnetic recording heads and storage media.

Standards

The National Measurement Institute of Germany's Physical Technical Federal Institute recently did an interlaboratory comparison of the step-height determination of AFMs and found a wide spread in measurement results. Standardization organizations including CEN/STAR and VAMAS worry that a lack of standards hampers the greater use of SPMs by industry. CEN/STAR is the European Committee for Standardization/Standardization and Research group, an organization that deals with new technologies.

VAMAS, the Versailles Project on Advanced Materials and Standards, was conceived by the world's leading economic nations, including the G7 countries and the European Union, to support world trade in products dependent on advanced materials technologies through international projects aimed at providing the technical basis for harmonized measurements, testing, specifications, and standards.

In June, standards experts from the United States, Europe, and Japan began discussing a strategy for new working groups on nanotechnology at a workshop at the National Physical Laboratory in Teddington, England. They proposed developing standards guidelines for SPM operations and tip calibration, and carrying out more interlaboratory comparisons of SPM measurements to calibrate instruments.

The development and evolution of SPMs has had a great impact on scientific and industrial research, and industry is beginning to explore and exploit the capabilities of these microscopes in quality control and production. The acceptance of SPMs for industrial uses should be further spurred with the development of SPM standards.

Reprinted with permission from *The Industrial Physicist*, 2002, American Institute of Physics

Imagine a bowl of light, holding a tiny collection of very cold atoms, one millionth of a degree above absolute zero. Now imagine that the

atoms are vibrating together as a single entity, creating a new state of matter like a small neutron star, sitting on a laboratory desktop. This fantastic-sounding piece of science fiction is a reality. It is made possible by carefully aiming intense laser beams at a group of atoms so that the electric field of the light exerts a force on the electrons and protons inside the atoms, optically trapping them inside a small cold "bowl."

John E. Thomas, professor of physics at Duke University, and Michael E. Gehm, a post-doctoral fellow at the same university, explain in this excerpt how they take advantage of the interaction forces between light and matter to create a Fermi gas, a gas so cold that quantum effects dominate and the atoms become a single entity, oscillating together in a single quantum wave state. —LCK

From "Optically Trapped Fermi Gases"
by John E. Thomas and Michael E. Gehm
American Scientist, May/June 2004

The bowl is only a millimeter long and a tenth of a millimeter wide, no bigger than a piece of lint. Its walls are constructed of pure light, making this "optical bowl" an appropriately ethereal container for the stuff sloshing around inside: lithium atoms that have been chilled to less than a millionth of a degree above absolute zero. But you shouldn't think of the sample trapped in this vessel of light as just a cloud of lithium (any more than you'd think of a diamond as a mere lump of carbon). Its value lies not in the atoms that make it up but in the special way they are put together—in a remarkable configuration known as a degenerate Fermi gas. Such an assemblage constitutes a new state of matter and is possibly the closest that scientists will ever come to having on their desktops a neutron star or a piece of the quark matter that made up the early universe.

Although physicists had predicted the existence of degenerate Fermi gases as long ago as the 1930s, nobody had produced a fully independent one in the lab until five years ago. The closest model we had was the cloud of electrons inside an ordinary metal like copper. Even though the metal is solid, the electrons behave very much like a gas: They are free to roam around (which makes the metal conduct electricity), but they have to fit into a strict energy hierarchy—the same one found in the degenerate Fermi gases we produced.

These gases are first cousins to another strange quantum beast that appears at ultracold temperatures, called a Bose-Einstein condensate. The research group of Eric Cornell and Carl Wieman at the University of Colorado at Boulder fashioned the first such condensate in 1995. (In 2001, Cornell and Wieman shared a Nobel prize for their work with Wolfgang Ketterle of the Massachusetts Institute of Technology.)

An atomic degenerate Fermi gas is even trickier to create, because it pits two precepts of quantum mechanics against each other. On the one hand is Heisenberg's famous uncertainty principle, which says that the location of any particle becomes more ambiguous as its speed becomes less uncertain. In an ultracold gas, the speed of the atoms is known with unusual precision: It is close to zero. Therefore the atoms get smeared out into blobs that are tens of thousands of times larger than a normal room-temperature atom. This blurring is no problem for a Bose-Einstein condensate, because it is made of "sociable" atoms called bosons, which like to overlap. But degenerate Fermi gases are made from solitary atoms called fermions (like the lithium in our trap), which according to Pauli's exclusion principle cannot share space with their neighbors. As a result, making a degenerate Fermi gas is a lot like trying to pack balloons into a closet. . .

Chilling Out with Lasers

The possibility of creating macroscopic quantum systems, such as degenerate Fermi gases and Bose-Einstein condensates, has come about largely because of improvements in the technology of optical cooling. In most experiments with ultracold gases, magnetic forces ensnare the atoms. By contrast, optical bowls use electric forces, which have the advantage that they can corral any kind of atom, whereas magnetic traps work only for certain types.

In the simplest case, an optical bowl consists of an intense laser beam that is tightly focused into a high-vacuum region. The light draws cold atoms or molecules toward its focal point and confines them in a frictionless, heat-free environment, which is ideal for studies of fundamental phenomena.

Why would a focused beam of light attract atoms? The secret is that light is an electromagnetic wave, consisting of oscillating electric and magnetic fields. The electric field in a light beam exerts a force on charged particles, such as the electrons and protons inside an atom. An atom, however, has an equal number of electrons and protons, and thus is electrically neutral. A force nonetheless arises, for a somewhat subtle reason: the field gradient.

If, for example, the electric field points upward and toward the focus of the beam, a positively charged nucleus in an atom below the beam will be pulled upward, and the negatively charged electron cloud will be pushed downward. The nucleus, being closer to the focus of the beam where the electric field is larger, then experiences an attraction that is slightly stronger than the repulsion the electron cloud feels, and so there is a net upward force on the atom. If the situation were reversed, with the electric field pointing away from the beam, the nucleus would move farther away, and the electron cloud would move closer. The net force would once again be toward the focus. For reasons that are too complicated to explain here, the same phenomenon holds for atoms on the axis of the beam, but located in front of or behind the focus. Thus, whichever direction the electric field points, the atom always gets pulled gently inward.

The key word here is "gently." At room temperature, or even well below, the random thermal movements of an atom will always overcome the feeble tug of the laser. Therefore, to capture atoms in an optical bowl, one has to use a very intense laser and make the atoms very

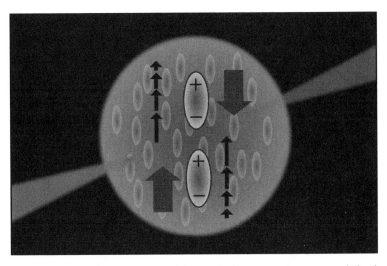

Trapping neutral atoms in a cold, rarefied gas can be accomplished using an "optical bowl," an intense laser that draws the atoms into the focus of the beam. The oscillating electric field of the laser causes the positively charged nucleus and the negatively charged electrons of each atom to become slightly separated. Because the electric field *(black arrows)* is greatest near the focus, the force on the positive side of an atom is not completely balanced by the opposing force on the negative side. Below the beam, for example, the upward force exerted on the top of an atom slightly exceeds the downward force on the bottom. Similarly, above the beam the downward force exerted on the bottom of an atom exceeds the upward force on the top. Thus in either case a net force arises, pulling the atoms inward.

cold, so they do not move too rapidly. The carbon dioxide laser in our experiments has an intensity at its focal point of 2 million watts per square centimeter, more than enough to cut through steel. Even at this intensity, the optical bowl is only deep enough to confine an atom whose initial temperature is less than a thousandth of a degree above absolute zero. . .

. . . Because the atoms have to be very cold already for us to capture them with a laser beam, setting up the optical bowl is the second part of our three-step protocol. First, we cool several hundred million lithium atoms down to about 150 millionths of a degree above absolute zero, using a now-standard strategy called a magneto-optical trap.

This device uses six red laser beams, arranged in three orthogonal pairs. Each of the pairs of beams slows the lithium atoms in a single direction by cleverly exploiting the Doppler effect. From the perspective of a moving atom, the laser beam that propagates in the opposite direction seems to shift to a higher frequency, and the atom will see this as an increased "headwind." At the same time, the laser beam that travels in the same direction as the atom will shift to a lower frequency and create a reduced "tailwind." Because the effect increases with the velocity of the atom, one can think of the laser light as exerting a viscous force. This is why one of the inventors of the magneto-optical trap, the Nobel laureate Steven Chu of Stanford University, coined the very appropriate nickname optical molasses.

Without the "molasses," an atom passing into our optical bowl would shoot right out again, like a marble dropped into a teacup from a considerable height. Having a magneto-optical trap is like filling the cup with honey first—the marble comes nearly to rest at the bottom of the bowl. Thus, we should be able to turn off the molasses after loading, and retain the atoms in the optical bowl for a very long time. . .

. . . After we confine the atoms in the bowl, they are still not cold enough for quantum effects to take over. For that, they need to be chilled even more using the third and final step, called evaporative cooling. There is nothing fancy about this stage; it is inspired by the way a hot bowl of soup cools. When two atoms collide, occasionally they can pool their energy, and one of them can gain enough oomph to escape the trap or "evaporate." The other one slows down. It then hits the other atoms in the trap, cooling them, and the process continues. Eventually the atoms get so cold that even two of them together do not have enough energy for one of them to leave. At this point no more evaporation can take place, and the cooling stagnates. To overcome this problem, we slowly lower the intensity of the trapping laser beam—in effect, lowering the "lip" of the optical bowl—so that some of the warmer atoms can escape. We lose about two-thirds of the atoms in this way, but the remaining ones become cold enough to form a degenerate Fermi gas.

Quantum Effects

According to quantum mechanics, all matter exhibits both particle-like and wavelike properties. When a particle, such as an electron or even a whole atom, is considered as a wave, it is said to have a "de Broglie wavelength," which determines the effective "size" of the particle. The de Broglie wavelength varies inversely with momentum. Increasing the momentum, as in a particle accelerator, makes the wavelength of the particle very small. . . When the momentum is very small, as in our optical trap, the atom spreads out like a balloon. At these extremely low temperatures, the balloon is about a micrometer in diameter—a length that is large enough to resolve with a good microscope.

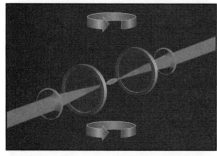

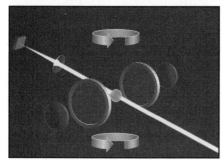

Formation and study of a degenerate Fermi gas begins with a cloud of lithium atoms, which are slowed by the six inward-directed laser beams of a magneto-optical trap *(top)*, a device that is said to create an "optical molasses." (The ringlike arrows indicate the flow of current in an adjacent pair of coils, which generates a magnetic field.) Once these atoms are cooled to 150 millionths of a degree above absolute zero, they can be confined in the "optical bowl" created by a single focused laser beam. Because the restoring force perpendicular to the beam is greater than along the beam, the bowl produces a cigar-shaped cloud of atoms *(center)*. Gradually decreasing the intensity of this beam allows some of the atoms to escape, cooling those that remain, which eventually reach 50 billionths of a degree above zero. At this temperature the gas becomes degenerate, a highly organized state that acts somewhat like a single "mega-atom." The authors study this phenomenon by turning off the laser that forms the optical bowl, allowing the cloud to expand. They obtain a sequence of pictures of the evolving cloud using short pulses of laser light *(bottom)*, which pass through the gas before being projected onto an imaging device. The behavior of the cloud as it expands preserves a "memory" of its time as a degenerate Fermi gas. *(Courtesy of Amy McDonald Turner)*

When the de Broglie wavelength gets large enough, the balloons start to touch one another and then try to overlap. At that point, the gas is called "degenerate," and its behavior starts to be governed by quantum rules rather than the rules of classical physics.

Yin and Yang

Since the 1930s, physicists have realized that quantum particles fall into two categories: bosons and fermions. Identical bosons are gregarious particles, preferring to occupy the same energy states as their neighbors. Photons (particles of light) behave this way, for example in lasers, where photons of a certain energy stimulate atoms to release more photons of the same energy.

The particles that make up ordinary matter— protons, neutrons, and electrons—are fermions, and they behave quite differently. As the physicists Enrico Fermi and P. A. M. Dirac discovered, these particles are introverts. Two fermions with the same "spin" cannot be at the same energy level and occupy the same region of space. (The spin of a particle has to do with the way it lines up in a magnetic field. It comes in two varieties: spin up and spin down.) This behavior, too, has major consequences in everyday life. It explains the periodic table. The second row of the periodic table, for instance, has eight elements because the second electron shell has slots for eight electrons. Two electrons can never share the same slot, because they are fermions.

Larger composite particles, such as atoms or molecules, act like fermions if they are made of an odd number of fermions, and like bosons if they are made up of an even number. Thus lithium-6, with 3 protons, 3 neutrons, and 3 electrons, is a composite fermion, whereas lithium-7, with one more neutron, is a composite boson. At ordinary temperatures the two isotopes have identical chemical properties, but at supercold temperatures, their different quantum personalities emerge.

When a gas of composite bosons, say one made up of lithium-7, is chilled in an optical bowl, a sudden transition occurs at the onset of degeneracy (the "transition temperature"). Suddenly the gas changes from a classical one, with the atoms in various energy states, to one in which they all have the same energy— the least that the container allows. That is, all of the atoms oscillate with the lowest energy and the longest wavelength possible. They vibrate in unison, like a single mega-atom. This is a Bose-Einstein condensate.

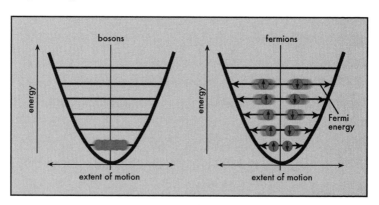

All atoms in a Bose-Einstein condensate attain the same energy level, the lowest one available *(left)*, whereas only two atoms (with opposite nuclear spin) can share one energy level in a degenerate Fermi gas *(right)*. As a result, the atoms in such a gas occupy a series of increasing energy levels, up to a level that corresponds to the Fermi temperature of the gas. The higher the energy level of an atom, the broader its oscillatory motion within the trap. *(Courtesy of Tom Dunne)*

When a gas of composite fermions, say one made up of lithium-6, is cooled to the transition temperature (called the "Fermi temperature" for fermions), a different transition takes place: The atoms begin to arrange themselves in an orderly fashion, two in the lowest energy state allowed, two in the next lowest, and so on—just as the electrons in a regular atom do. The result is a degenerate Fermi gas, which might be thought of as a different kind of mega-atom.

Soon after Cornell and Wieman created the first Bose-Einstein condensate, investigators began trying to produce the first degenerate Fermi gas of atoms. . . In 1999, Deborah Jin of the University of Colorado succeeded with potassium-40, using a modified version of Cornell and Wieman's magnetic trapping techniques. Unfortunately, Jin's method does not apply to all atoms, and it took other groups a longer time to develop more general techniques. In 2001 Randy Hulet's group at Rice University, Christophe Salomon's at École Normale Supérieure, and Ketterle's at MIT achieved success using magnetically trapped bosons to cool fermions contained in the same trap. Hulet and Salomon showed that fermionic lithium-6 gas occupies a much larger volume than bosonic lithium-7. This difference makes sense, because the fermions are forced to adopt many different energy levels—and some thus must move in orbits of large radius, whereas the bosons all crowd into the lowest energy state and have a small radius of motion.

At the same time, our group at Duke also managed to produce degenerate Fermi gases colder than one-tenth of the Fermi temperature, using all-optical cooling methods.

Reprinted with permission from *American Scientist*, © 2004, Written by John E. Thomas, Michael E. Gehm

There are only four fundamental forces in the universe: electromagnetic, gravitational, strong, and weak. On the scale of our everyday world, we are only directly aware of the electromagnetic force, which we harness in motors, for example, and the gravitational force, which helps keep our feet firmly rooted to the ground. The strong and weak forces are responsible for the integrity of every nucleus in the universe, acting only in the small distances inside those very tiny collections of particles. When engineers and scientists began to create small machines with parts that are about one-millionth of a meter in size, still much larger than any nucleus, they found that only the electromagnetic force had any significant effect on those parts.

Micromachines, known as MEMS (micro-electromechanical systems), are minuscule but wonderful machines that are capable of perform-ing tirelessly in an endlessly imaginative variety of applications. MEMS are created using the same technology used to create the technological basis of modern computing: the silicon chip. These little machines have components that interact with each other through electromagnetic force, sometimes through the quantum mechanical manifestation of that force. Researchers at Bell Labs, Lucent Technologies, and Agere Systems, all in Murray Hill, New Jersey, explain in this article excerpt how forces act differently on the macroscopic and microscopic scales and describe some of the fascinating applications of MEMS. —LCK

From "The Little Machines That Are Making It Big"
by David Bishop, Peter Gammel, and C. Randy Giles
Physics Today, October 2001

Imagine a world with machines the size of mites tending to all sorts of jobs. Some of them keep cars running smoothly and safely, saving hundreds of thousands of people from perishing in auto accidents. Other machines rout petabits (peta $= 10^{15}$) of information each second, play movies downloaded from the World Wide Web, or perform scientific measurements of an unprecedented sensitivity and precision. Chip-sized chemical factories produce dangerous materials, but only when and where needed.

Such a world exists today: We live in it. It is the world of modern silicon micromechanics.[1] This world was anticipated with remarkable foresight by Richard Feynman more than 40 years ago, when transistors were a new and unproven technology and integrated circuits

(ICs) were still many years into the future. In his 1959 talk, "There's Plenty of Room at the Bottom," published shortly thereafter,[2] Feynman suggested what micromachines could be, why one would want to use them, how to build them, and how physics for machines at the microscale would be different than for machines at the macroscale. Nowadays, it is possible to fabricate inexpensive micromachines that range in size from 0.1 to 100 microns, require little power, and operate at high speed. Such qualities make micromachines a compelling choice for a wide variety of applications. Micromechanics technology is profoundly changing the way we think about and use machines.

True Machines

The microscopic devices we are talking about are machines in the truest sense of the word. They have moving parts, sometimes millions of them. They can be as simple as cantilevers or as complicated as mechanical clocks. Elements such as rotary joints, springs, hinged plates, simple screws, suspended and unsuspended beams, diaphragms, mechanical striplines, and latches can be built and used reliably in a wealth of applications.

Micromachines, or microelectromechanical systems (MEMS), are made using a variety of techniques originally developed for use in the $200-billion-per-year semiconductor industry. Sophisticated deposition tools, lithographic processes, wire bonders, photoresists, packages, Si wafers, modeling tools, and even reliability methodologies can be used in making MEMS devices. The benefit of being able to recycle existing technologies cannot be overestimated; recycling can be especially useful for those who design devices intended primarily for scientific applications, typically with almost no development funds.

The worldwide market for MEMS is estimated to exceed tens of billions of dollars in the next several years. In this article, we will focus on a number of key application areas: automobiles, handheld phones, display technologies, lightwave systems, and scientific measurements.

Car Talk

An important, commercially successful MEMS device in widespread use today is the automotive airbag sensor[3] which measures rapid deceleration of a car and triggers the explosive filling of an airbag. Before the use of a MEMS device in this application, airbags were typically triggered by an electromechanical device roughly the size of a can of soda, weighing several pounds and costing about $15. Now the same function is accomplished with a MEMS device that costs just a few dollars and is the size of a small cube of sugar. The smaller size of the MEMS device allows it to respond more quickly to rapid deceleration. As a consequence, it is now practical to have airbags in car doors to protect occupants against side impacts. MEMS airbag sensors have an additional important advantage over their macromechanical predecessors—integrated electronics that allow for self-testing. The test is initiated whenever a driver turns on the ignition, and its successful conclusion is indicated by an illuminated dashboard light.

Other applications for MEMS in automobiles include inertial sensors for keeping track of a car's location, tilt meters to warn of impending roll-overs, and pressure gauges used in the engine to assure proper and efficient operation. In the near future, MEMS devices will be key components of smart tires, which will remain properly inflated at all times. If tires are maintained with proper air pressure, not only will cars be safer, but, in addition, the US could reduce fuel consumption by an estimated 10%. Smart tires have microscopic pressure sensors as part of a feedback loop that includes a pump in the car. Thus, the responsibility of maintaining proper tire pressure rests with the car, not with the driver.

Automotive applications mark the beginning of a radically new technology. The airbag sensor in particular, with its better than 100 million device years of experience in the inhospitable environment of a car, has proved the reliability of this technology. The experience gained in the automotive arena can be used to guide the application of MEMS devices in other equally demanding environments. . .

Scientific Measurements

We believe that MEMS devices are likely to play an increasingly important role in making scientific measurements. When one of us (DJB) was a student at Cornell University more than a few years ago, experimentalists were all sent off to the student shop to learn how to drill and turn and mill and tap metals so that they could build macroexperimental equipment.

Students can now use computers and computer-aided design tools to help build micromachines used in their labs' scientific experiments. The files that they write on a personal computer get sent out to a "fab," where the devices they have designed are made and then shipped to the lab. Some have coined the phrase "the new physics machine shop" to describe the fabrication of micromachines for experiments in basic science. For the students taking this new approach, an ion mill is a more important tool than the metal mill many of us were taught to use when we were students. Both mills do the same job, but on very different length scales.

The art of scientific measurement is to achieve high accuracy and precision in the face of limited funds. MEMS devices are beginning to find numerous applications in this area. Examples include high-sensitivity magnetometers, micromachines that measure the Casimir force, calorimeters, bolometers, adaptive optics for astronomy and vision science,[8] and devices for studying mesoscopic vortex physics. Here we consider high-sensitivity magnetometers and the measurement of the Casimir force.

High-Sensitivity Magnetometers

One of the most important properties of a solid-state material is its magnetization. MEMS devices provide a powerful new probe of this property, and are especially useful in the extreme limit of very high magnetic fields.

In recent years, experimental condensed matter physicists have developed a way to generate magnetic fields with a strength of about 75 tesla. These fields, however, only last for a few milliseconds. MEMS magnetometers, using a microscopic Faraday balance, are able to measure the magnetization of a material in this brief period.[9] The balance looks like a small trampoline. It is part of a capacitor, connected to a sensitive bridge circuit that allows small changes in the trampoline's displacement to be measured. A sample weighing roughly 1 microgram is glued to the balance and is placed in a pulsed magnet in a region where the field is reasonably high and the field gradient is nonvanishing. The sample is subject to a force proportional to the field gradient times the magnetization of the sample. By knowing the trampoline's spring constant, one can relate the displacement of the trampoline to changes in the magnetization as the sample responds to the rapidly varying magnetic field. . .

Casimir Force Measurements

The Casimir force exists between two uncharged metal surfaces due to zero-point fluctuations of the electromagnetic vacuum. It is a purely quantum-mechanical effect, predicted by Hendrick Casimir in 1948. Unlike the Coulomb interaction, which varies inverse quadratically with distance, the Casimir force varies inversely as the fourth power (for planar conducting surfaces; in general, the force depends on geometry). Plates separated by 10 nm are subject to a Casimir pressure of about one atmosphere, but the Casimir force falls off so rapidly with distance that the gravitational and Casimir forces are roughly comparable for plates separated by as little as a micron. . .

The Casimir effect has been exploited in the building of hysteric oscillators. In the future, the effect will enable construction of a new generation of exquisitely sensitive position sensors. In a very real sense, MEMS devices allow one to use a force created out of the vacuum.

A Lesson from an Old Radio

In this article we have given the reader a mere glimpse of what has been done with MEMS devices and what may be accomplished in the near future. It is clear to us that the field of micromechanics will change the paradigm of what machines are, how and where we use them, what they cost, and how we design them. It may not be an exaggeration to say that we are on the verge of a new industrial revolution driven by a new and completely different class of machines.

The invention of the transistor may prove a useful guide for what to expect. When first discovered, the transistor was used as a replacement for vacuum tubes in applications, like radios, where vacuum tubes worked well enough. One of us (DJB) recalls that, in 1960, he received as a birthday gift a transistor radio whose case proudly announced that the radio had six transistors. Six-transistor radios would have been easy to predict in 1947 when the transistor was invented. Today, however, we take for granted microprocessors with tens of millions of transistors. No one in 1947 could have predicted such a thing and what it would do to our world.

We currently use micromachines to do things that in most cases can be done by macromachines. (The micromachines, however, do a better job.) In 20 or 30 years, though, society will be using micromachines in ways impossible for us to imagine today. Those of us working in the field of micromechanics look forward to helping make it happen.

How Is Micromechanics Different?

One of the charms of working in the microworld is that mechanics can be quite different at the microscopic scale from what we experience at the macroscopic scale of daily life: One has to develop a whole new intuition about mechanical things. In the microworld some things are the same as in our world, some are quite different, and the fun is figuring it all out.

The main difference in the microworld is that the surface area to volume ratio is very different from that for mechanical devices in the macroworld, so the relative importance of inertia and friction are different, and surface effects can be important.

We who live at a macroscopic scale notice the effects of inertia every day. Balls keep rolling after being pushed. Birds glide. Swimmers coast to the edge of a swimming pool. Friction is important but not dominant. However, at the microscale, the relative importance of friction and inertia switch. Friction dominates. Even if it were as smart as Newton, a paramecium would never be able to discover inertia—it stops dead in its tracks the instant it stops swimming.

For micromachines, surface effects are paramount. For example, one can build devices that change their overall mechanical response due to a phase transition in a single monolayer on the surface.

Another interesting effect becomes prominent at the microscale, something called stiction, a composite of "sticky" and "friction." At the microscale, molecular attractions can overwhelm restoring forces for simple objects. When tiny objects touch, for example, they can get stuck forever. One has to worry about whether a simple cantilever (a beam supported at one end, like a diving board) will ever come back up after its end touches down.

Two types of stiction are worrisome. The first is release stiction. This type arises because the final step in the fabrication of micromachines, called the release step, often uses wet chemistry. If one is not careful, surface tension can pull things together as the liquid dries. (Think of two wet pieces of paper.) A standard solution to this difficulty is to use supercritical drying, which, by going around the critical point, avoids going across a liquid-vapor phase line and having a meniscus to worry about.

The other type of stiction is in-use stiction, where elements of a micromachine get stuck together if they are allowed to touch. Techniques to defeat in-use stiction range from using dimples and fingers to minimize contact area, to applying very elaborate nonstick coatings. At the microscopic scale, water is an effective glue that will gum up the operation of a micromachine. Commercial devices use hermetic, waterproof packages to resolve this problem.

Another interesting difference between macroscopic and microscopic devices is the nature of the forces that move things around. At macroscopic scales, electromagnetic forces tend to be used to build strong motors. Magnets and coils of wire with currents in them can produce large forces. In the macroworld, electrostatic forces are mainly useful for amusements like sticking balloons to a wall. At the microscale, things are different. For a fixed current density in a wire, electromagnetic forces get smaller when the sizes of wires and magnets scale down, while electrostatic forces can become large enough to be practical as objects get closer together. Therefore, electrostatic actuation is a standard technique for micromachines while it's seldom used for macromachines.

Other interesting effects that are safely ignored at macroscopic scales can become important in the microworld, including quantized thermal conductance, Brownian motion, mesoscopic mechanical properties, and exotic dislocation line motions. Life is very interesting in the microworld and we are just beginning to find out how different it is.

References

1. For a general reference on micromachines in a wide range of applications, see the special issue on "Microelectromechanical Systems: Technology and Applications," *MRS Bull.* **26** (April 2001).
2. R. Feynman, *Eng. Sci.* **23**, 22 (1960).
3. T. A. Core, W. K. Tsang, S. J. Sherman, *Solid State Technol.* **36**, 39 (1993).
8. For more information on adaptive optics, see the Center for Adaptive Optics Web site at http://cfao.ucolick.org/.
9. V. Aksyuk *et al.*, *Science* **280**, 720 (1998).
10. C. Bolle *et al.*, *Nature* **399**, 43 (1999).
11. H. B. Chan *et al.*, *Science* **291**, 1941 (2001).

Reprinted with permission from American Institute of Physics, © 2001
Authors: David Bishop, Peter Gammel, and C. Randy Giles

Current Research on Electromagnetism

4

The unquenchable thirst of the marketplace for new technology has spurred research all over the world, in many different fields. There just doesn't seem to be any areas that remain unexplored, yet new ideas continually crop up, such as the brighter and more efficient electronic displays offered by light-emitting organic materials.

Stephen R. Forrest, a professor of electrical engineering at Princeton University, describes in this article excerpt how that search is developing in a field that combines two unlikely partners of the technological future: organic materials, complex polymers in this case, and inorganic materials, such as glass, plastic, or metal. The two groups of materials seem incompatible, combining fragile but flexible organic materials, which cling to any substrate with a weak force, with robust materials to create applications like film displays and photovoltaic cells. Yet there are already thin-film organic devices available, and there certainly will be more applications in the future. —LCK

From "The Path to Ubiquitous and Low-Cost Organic Electronic Appliances on Plastic"
by Stephen R. Forrest
Nature, April 29, 2004

Organic electronics are beginning to make significant inroads into the commercial world, and if the field continues to progress at its current, rapid pace, electronics based on organic thin-film materials will soon become a mainstay of our technological existence. Already products based on active thin-film organic devices are in the market place, most notably the displays of several mobile electronic appliances. Yet the future holds even greater promise for this technology, with an entirely new generation of ultralow-cost, lightweight and even flexible electronic devices in the offing, which will perform functions traditionally accomplished using much more expensive components based on conventional semiconductor materials such as silicon.

Interest in organic electronics stems from the ability to deposit organic films on a variety of very-low-cost substrates such as glass, plastic or metal foils, and the relative ease of processing of the organic compounds that are currently being engineered by hundreds of chemists. The most advanced organic electronic systems already in commercial production are high-efficiency, very bright and colourful thin displays based on organic light-emitting devices (OLEDs).[1] Significant progress is also being made in the realization of thin-film transistors (TFTs)[2-4] and thin-film organic photovoltaic cells[5-8] for low-cost solar energy generation. Yet the ultimate test of this technology lies less in the reliability and performance of the organic components, which in some cases has already approached or even exceeded the requirements of a particular application, but rather in the ability to manufacture products at very low-cost. Although the cost of the organic materials used in most thin-film devices is low, in electronics the materials cost rarely determines that of the end product, where fabrication and packaging costs typically dominate. Hence, the successful application of this interesting materials platform will depend on capturing its low-cost potential through the innovative fabrication of devices on inexpensive, large-area substrates.

This suggests that conventional semiconductor device fabrication technologies need to be adapted to handle the large-area substrates spanned by organic macroelectronic circuits, and to be compatible with the physical and chemical properties of these fascinating compounds. Also, solids based on organic compounds are typically bonded by weak van der Waals forces that decrease as $1/R^6$, where R is the intermolecular spacing. This is in contrast to inorganic semiconductors that are covalently bonded, whose strength falls off as $1/R^2$. Hence, organic electronic materials are soft and fragile, whereas inorganic semiconductors are hard, brittle, and relatively robust when exposed to adverse environmental agents such as moisture and the corrosive reagents and plasmas commonly used in device fabrication. The apparent fragility of organic materials has also opened the door to a suite of innovative fabrication methods that are simpler to implement on a large scale than has been thought possible in the world of inorganic semiconductors. Many processes involve direct printing through use of contact with stamps, or alternatively via ink-jets and other solution-based methods.

Here I describe several recent advances in organic electronic devices, focusing particularly on the specialized processing techniques used in their realization. The discussion begins with a description of the unique electronic and optical properties of organic materials that make them interesting as technological substances. This is followed by a discussion of the methods of film deposition and patterning using techniques that have been developed to maintain the very low costs inherent in these material systems. The promise of organic electronics through the production of ubiquitous, low-cost, and robust devices filling niches not occupied by silicon-based electronics should become readily apparent through the understanding of the unique properties that characterize these potentially high-performance materials.

Essential Properties of Organic Semiconductors

Like all organic materials, organic semiconductors are carbon-rich compounds with a structure tailored to optimize a particular function, such as charge mobility or luminescent properties. Organic electronic materials (Fig. 1, page 123) can be classified into three categories: "small molecules," polymers, and biological materials. "Small molecule" is a term broadly used to refer to those compounds with a well-defined molecular weight.

The material shown, Pt-octaethylporphyrin (PtOEP), is a metallorganic complex that has been optimized to provide deep red phosphorescent emission when placed in an OLED.[9] Other small-molecular-weight materials include low-generation dendrimers and other oligomers.[10, 11] In contrast, polymers are long-chain molecules consisting of an indeterminate number of molecular repeat units. The molecule shown is poly (p-phenylene vinylene), or PPV. Like PtOEP, PPV is an emissive organic semiconductor used in OLEDs.[12-14] At the high end of the complexity scale are organic materials of biological origin (in contrast to PtOEP and PPV, which are synthetic). As yet there are no clear applications that exploit the optical or electronic properties of these most complicated structures, although considerable investigation into the understanding and utilization of

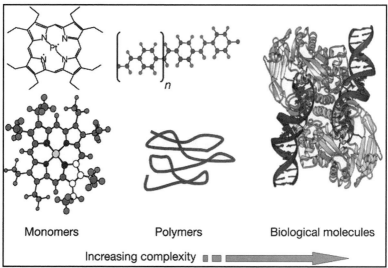

Monomers   Polymers   Biological molecules

Increasing complexity

Figure 1. Various types of organic electronic materials, ranged in order of increasing complexity from left (simplest) to right (most complex).

photosynthetic complexes is currently under way.[15, 16] This review concerns only monomeric and polymeric materials, as they are in the most advanced state of development for electronic and photonic applications.

Although much emphasis has been placed on the differences between the properties of small-molecular-weight organic thin films and polymers for organic electronic applications, there are in general more similarities than differences in both their electronic and optical properties, with the main distinction being in the methods of thin-film deposition and device preparation. In both polymers and small molecules, the excitonic state dominates their optical properties.[17] Here, an exciton is a molecular excited state that is mobile within the solid—that is, it can hop from molecule to molecule, or in the case of polymers, from chain to chain as well as along the polymer backbone until it recombines, generating either light (in a radiative process) or heat (under non-radiative circumstances).

The most dominant species in organic electronic devices is the Frenkel exciton—a tightly bound (1-eV binding energy) electron–hole pair that is generally localized on a single molecule at a time.[18] In addition, in highly ordered molecular crystals, more weakly bound charge-transfer (CT) excitons are found in the optical spectra. These equally mobile states are generally spread over one or more neighbouring molecules, and owing to their larger diameters, are more weakly bound (10–100 meV) than Frenkel states.

Similarly, charge carrier (electron or hole) transport can occur via hopping between molecular sites, or from chain to chain. In this case, the carrier mobilities are quite low compared with inorganic semiconductors whose room temperature values typically range from 100 to 104 cm^2 V-1 s-1.[19] In contrast, in highly ordered molecular materials where charges hop between closely spaced molecules forming a crystalline stack, mobilities of μ 1 cm^2 V-1 s-1 have been observed at room temperature.[20-22] This apparently is an approximate upper bound, with the mobility ultimately limited by thermal motion between neighbouring molecules. In more disordered molecular systems and polymers, the mobilities are only 10^{-3} to 10^{-5} times this upper limit.[23-25] However, deposition (generally by spinning) of polymers onto substrates prepared by rubbing or other "direction-inducing" processes can lead to alignment of the chains, thus increasing the charge mobility over that of completely randomly disordered films.[26] A further strategy for reducing disorder in molecular systems as well as in polymers is by templating ordered epitaxy-like growth using crystalline substrates that impose their lattice order onto the adsorbed organic films.[27, 28] However, this latter approach may also result in a prohibitive increase of device fabrication complexity, or may be limited to only a few organic materials and substrates that are not necessarily optimal for use in a particular application. . .

. . . Owing to the low conductivity and carrier velocities that are intrinsic to organic thin-film semi-conductors, one would expect that very-low-bandwidth operation of common optoelectronic devices such as transistors, OLEDs and photodetectors would provide a significant, if not fatal, limitation to their application in modern electronic systems. Although in many cases this is indeed true, the applications open to organic electronics are not targeted at simply replacing conventional electronics niches served by materials such as crystalline silicon. For example, very-low-bandwidth (10-kHz) organic thin-film transistors (OTFTs) may find application in display back planes or low-cost "disposable" electronics, such as building entry cards and other radio-frequency identification inventory control.[31, 32] In addition, by using the thin vertical dimension (normal to the substrate plane) and the high crystalline order inherent in some molecular thin-film systems, very short carrier transit distances, and hence response times, can be obtained, leading to surprisingly high bandwidths. This has recently been demonstrated using multiple-layer organic photodetectors with bandwidths approaching 450 MHz.[33] Further possibilities for exploiting the short vertical dimensions have also been demonstrated in polymer OTFTs by depositing polythiophene derivatives into a "V"-shaped channel microcut into a flexible poly (ethylene terephthalate) substrate.[34]

The viability of organic electronics, therefore, lies not in the displacement of existing applications niches currently filled by conventional semiconductors, per se, but rather in capturing the low cost and enormous variability inherent in organic systems that are otherwise not accessible. Success in achieving very-low-cost electronics hinges almost entirely on the ability to deposit and fabricate organic electronic devices using methods that represent a revolutionary departure from those commonly used by the current high-performance

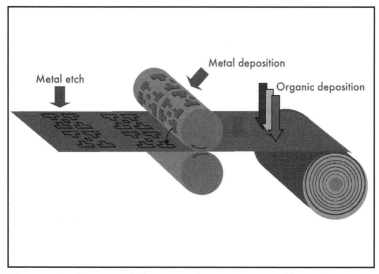

Figure 7. Conceptual diagram of continuous and low-cost manufacture of organic electronic devices.

electronics industry. Hence, a great deal of current research has focused on depositing films and patterning devices on a large scale (leading to "macroelectronic" applications), avoiding the need for labour-intensive techniques such as photolithography that today dominate the cost structure of conventional electronics. . .

The Organic Future

The opportunities for the use of organic thin films in modern electronic circuits are rapidly expanding, based on the very high-performance and unique functionality offered by these principally carbon-containing semiconductors. However, their practical implementation in electronic applications will ultimately be decided by the ability to produce devices and circuits at a cost that is significantly below that needed to manufacture conventional electronic circuits based on, for example, silicon. If successful, these low-cost fabrication processes will ultimately result in the "printing" of large-area organic electronic circuits using roll-to-roll or web-based methods, where low-temperature deposition of the organics is followed by metal deposition and patterning in a continuous, high-speed process analogous, perhaps, to processes used in the printing of documents or fabrics (Fig. 7, page 127). However, much work must be done before such an ambitious goal can be realized. Although many innovative technologies have been developed relating to the fabrication of thin-film organic devices with high performance and long operational lifetime, very few of these technologies have left the laboratory and found their way into a manufacturing environment. Indeed, only the simplest fabrication technologies have so far been implemented on manufacturing lines: spin-coating of polymers over broad substrate surfaces to create monochrome displays, or in the case of small molecules, vacuum deposition through shadow masks resulting in full colour displays. Yet even these early demonstrations are impressive. As the more sophisticated and versatile methods currently being developed in the laboratory make their way into the manufacturing environment, we can expect that organic electronic circuits whose functions are only now being envisioned will one day revolutionize the technological world in which we live.

End Notes

1. Vaeth, K. M. OLED-display technology. *Inform. Display* **19**, 12–17 (2003).

2. Lin, Y. Y., Gundlach, D. J., Nelson, S. F. & Jackson, T. N. in *55th Annu. Dev. Res. Conf.* **60** (Electron Device Society, Ft Collins, Colorado, 1997).

3. Gundlach, D. J., Lin, Y. Y. & Jackson, T. N. Pentacene organic thin film transistors-molecular ordering and mobility. *IEEE Electron. Dev. Lett.* **18,** 87–89 (1997) Article ISI ChemPort.

4. Shtein, M., Mapel, J., Benziger, J. B. & Forrest, S. R. Effects of film morphology and gate dielectric surface preparation on the electrical characteristics of organic vapor phase deposited pentacene thin-film transistors. *Appl. Phys. Lett.* **81,** 268–270 (2002) Article ISI ChemPort.

5. Peumans, P. & Forrest, S. R. Very high efficiency double heterostructure copper phthalocyanine/C60 photovoltaic cells. *Appl. Phys. Lett.* **79,** 126–128 (2001) Article ISI ChemPort.

6. Granstrom, M. *et al.* Laminated fabrication of polymeric photovoltaic diodes. *Nature* **395,** 257–260 (1998) Article ISI ChemPort.

7. Peumans, P., Uchida, S. & Forrest, S. R. Efficient bulk heterojunction photovoltaic cells based on small molecular weight organic thin films. *Nature* **425,** 158–162 (2003) Article PubMed ISI ChemPort.

8. Shaheen, S. E. et al. 2.5 % efficient organic plastic solar cells. *Appl. Phys. Lett.* **78,** 841-843 (2001) Article ISI ChemPort.

9. Baldo, M. A. et al. High efficiency phosphorescent emission from organic electroluminescent devices. *Nature* **395,** 151–154 (1998) Article ISI ChemPort.

10. Anthopoulos, T. D. et al. Highly efficient single-layer dendrimer light-emitting diodes with balanced charge transport. *Appl. Phys. Lett.* **82,** 4824–4826 (2003) Article ISI ChemPort.

11. Ma, D. G. *et al.* Bright electroluminescence from a new conjugated dendrimer. *Synth. Met.* **137,** 1125–1126 (2003) Article ISI ChemPort.

12. Lee, C.-L., Lee, K. B. & Kim, J.-J. Polymer phosphorescent light emitting devices doped with tris (2-phenylpyridine) iridium as a triplet emitter. *Appl. Phys. Lett.* **77,** 2280–2282 (2000) Article ISI ChemPort.

13. Burroughes, J. H. et al. Light-emitting diodes based on conjugated polymers. *Nature* **347,** 539–541 (1990) Article ISI ChemPort.

14. Braun, D. & Heeger, A. J. Visible light emission from semiconducting polymer diodes. *Appl. Phys. Lett.* **58,** 1982–1984 (1991) Article ISI ChemPort.

15. Greenbaum, E., Blankinship, S. L., Lee, J. W. & Ford, R. M. Solar photobiochemistry: Simultaneous photoproduction of hydrogen and oxygen in a confined bioreactor. *J. Phys. Chem.* **B 105,** 3605–3609 (2001) Article ISI ChemPort.

16. Greenbaum, E., Lee, I. & Lee, J. W. Functional 3D nanoscale imaging of a single-molecule photovoltaic structure. *Biophys. J. Part 2* **82,** 206–207 (2002).

17. Pope, M. & Swenberg, C. E. *Electronic Processes in Organic Crystals* (Clarendon, Oxford, 1982).

18. Silinsh, E. A. in Organic Molecular Crystals (ed. Queisser, H.-J.) Ch. 1 (Springer, Berlin, 1980).

19. Sze, S. M. *Physics of Semiconductor Devices* (John Wiley, New York, 1981).

20. Warta, W., Stehle, R. & Karl, N. Ultrapure, high mobility organic photo-conductors. *Appl. Phys.* **A 36**, 163–170 (1985) ISI.

21. Karl, N. Studies of organic semiconductors for 40 years. III. *Mol. Cryst. Liq. Cryst.* **171**, 31–51 (1989) ISI.

22. Forrest, S. R., Kaplan, M. L. & Schmidt, P. H. Organic-on-inorganic semi-conductor contact barrier diodes. II. Dependence on organic film and metal contact properties. *J. Appl. Phys.* **56**, 543–551 (1984) Article ISI ChemPort.

23. Campbell, A. J., Bradley, D. D. C. & Antoniadis, H. Dispersive electron transport in an electroluminescent polyfluorene copolymer measured by the current integration time-of-flight method. *Appl. Phys. Lett.* **79**, 2133–2135 (2001) Article ISI ChemPort.

24. Blom, P. W. M., de Jong, M. J. M. & vanMunster, M. G. Electric-field and temperature dependence of the hole mobility in poly (p-phenylene vinylene). *Phys. Rev.* **B 55**, R656–R659 (1997) Article ISI ChemPort

25. Bulovic, V., Burrows, P. E. & Forrest, S. R. in *Electroluminescence I* (ed. Mueller, G.) 262 (Academic, New York, 2000).

26. Sirringhaus, H. *et al.* Mobility enhancement in conjugated polymer field-effect transistors through chain alignment in a liquid-crystalline phase. *Appl. Phys. Lett.* **77**, 406–408 (2000) Article ISI ChemPort.

27. Forrest, S. R. Ultrathin organic films grown by organic molecular beam deposition and related techniques. *Chem. Rev.* **97**, 1793–1896 (1997) Article PubMed ISI ChemPort.

28. van de Craats, A. M. et al. Meso-epitaxial solution-growth of self organizing discotic liquid-crystalline semiconductors. *Adv. Mat.* **15**, 495–499 (2003) Article ISI ChemPort.

31. Gelinck, G. H., Geuns, T. C. T. & de Leeuw, D. M. High-performance all-polymer integrated circuits. Appl. Phys. Lett. 77, 1487–1489 (2000) Article ISI ChemPort.

32. Drury, C. J., Mutsaers, C. M. J., Hart, C. M., Matters, M. & de Leeuw, D. M. Low-cost all-polymer integrated circuits. *Appl. Phys. Lett.* **73**, 108–110 (1998) Article ISI ChemPort.

33. Peumans, P., Bulovic, V. & Forrest, S. R. Efficient, high-bandwidth organic multilayer photodetectors. *Appl. Phys. Lett.* **76**, 3855–3857 (2000) Article ISI ChemPort.

34. Stutzmann, N., Friend, R. H. & Sirringhaus, H. Self-aligned vertical-channel polymer field effect transistors. *Science* **299**, 1881–1884 (2003) Article PubMed ISI ChemPort.

Reprinted with permission from *Nature*. Fig. 1 courtesy of *Nature*. Fig. 7, courtesy of Tom Jackson

Every bit of wire used in every home, industry, commercial shop, or school wastes energy. It is unavoidable in the process that the current passing through a wire dissipates energy, converting electrical energy into heat that wastefully radiates away. Or is it? It is possible to pass current through superconducting wires without losing energy to heat, but only under a specific condition: in temperatures that are too cold for humans to survive.

Superconductivity has been around in the scientific world since 1911, but it burst onto the mainstream science scene in 1987, during the March meeting of the American Physical Society, the "Woodstock of physics." When the world's physicists gathered together that year, they were excited to be witnesses to a historical event, the announcement of the discovery of "high temperature" superconductivity in some carefully crafted ceramics. At the reasonably low temperature where air liquefies, these ceramics lose all resistance to electrical current. Although the temperatures cited for the transition to superconductivity were still very cold, the excitement was about the potential to produce room temperature superconductors. Science writer Barnaby J. Feder reports on what happened after that, how scientists and engineers are pushing research on the high temperature superconductors toward commercial products that will deliver magnetically levitating trains

*and inexpensive superconducting wire for
power generators, transformers, and transmission lines. —LCK*

"The Biggest Jolt to Power Since Franklin Flew His Kite"
by Barnaby J. Feder
The New York Times, April 27, 2004

In a onetime printing plant on the edge of this tattered
manufacturing city, a small company named Superpower
churns out sample after sample of what looks like shiny
metal tape.

The tape has five layers. The middle one, a
ceramic film one-tenth as thick as a human hair,
exhibits one of nature's most tantalizing tricks. At
very low temperatures, the ceramic abruptly loses all
resistance to electrical current.

That free-flowing current generates a strong magnetic
field, a feature that Superpower technicians demonstrate
by showing visitors how a thumbnail-size magnet floats
half an inch or so above a ribbon of chilled tape.

Superconductivity, as the phenomenon is known,
has fascinated and baffled scientists since its discovery
in 1911. Even now, they have yet to develop a compre-
hensive theory to explain its appearance in materials as
diverse as metal and ceramics.

Such scientific conundrums are of only passing
interest at Superpower, a four-year-old subsidiary of
Intermagnetics General, and at other companies like it.
After years of false starts and setbacks, these companies

say they are closing in on the goal of producing relatively inexpensive superconducting wire for power generators, transformers and transmission lines.

Success requires making yard after yard of wire, and eventually mile after mile. The focus at the companies, at national laboratories and at many universities is on questions that call for a genius like Edison than Einstein.

"We are finding out what works and going with that," said Dr. Jodi L. Reeves, a senior materials scientist at Superpower.

Success could spring superconductivity from the modest niches that it has occupied in fields like medical diagnostics and give it wide commercial applications. In addition to cutting costs and raising reliability in generating and distributing electricity, superconductive wire could replace copper wire in motors to save space and cut energy costs in factories and on ships. Railroads might finally embrace maglev technology, which allows high-speed trains to ride magnetic fields above superconductive rails.

The alloys used in medical imaging superconduct only at supercold temperatures, about 450 degrees below zero Fahrenheit. To reach that point, they have to be cooled by liquid helium, which is expensive to make and manage.

By contrast, ceramic superconductors work at temperatures above minus 321 Fahrenheit, allowing them to be cooled by liquid nitrogen, an inexpensive industrial refrigerant. For that reason, they are called high-temperature superconductors, though they are still far from the dream of a room-temperature superconductor.

The first reports of ceramic superconductors, in 1986, touched off a global research race to understand them and find others. The excitement peaked at the annual meeting of the American Physical Society in March 1987, when thousands of researchers crowded into a hastily organized midnight presentation.

That session, later called the Woodstock of physics, ran for hours as research groups from around the world reported their successes, sometimes with data updated to include results just hours old.

For some who were there, it was a life-altering experience. Dr. Gregory J. Yurek, a professor of materials science and engineering at the Massachusetts Institute of Technology, founded a company called American Superconductor in his kitchen in Wellesley, Mass., and resigned his tenured position the next year to work full time on his fledgling business. Experts from Intermagnetics General, a manufacturer of superconducting metals that was spun out of General Electric in 1971, immediately began work on the materials.

"Superconductivity was guaranteed to be a field where everything you did would be new," said Dr. Venkat Selvamanickam, who joined the first wave of research as a graduate student at the University of Houston, home to one of the leading high-temperature superconductivity research groups. He was hired by Intermagnetics in 1996 to lead the development work that it handed off to Superpower.

Although the United States and other countries have poured hundreds of millions of dollars into the area, success has not been quick. Unlike metal superconductors, the ceramic ones are naturally brittle and powdery. There was no simple process to transform them into wire.

Moreover, superconductivity in ceramic tape is easily disrupted by magnetic flux, in which changes in the magnetic field drift through the superconducting layers of the tape likes swirling weather systems through the atmosphere. Figuring how to immobilize the magnetic vortices, and atomic-scale process called pinning, has emerged as a crucial area for research.

Early ceramic compounds were based on bismuth. The complexity of manufacturing and the need to rely on silver substrates to provide a workable mix of strength and stability to the bismuth compounds kept costs so much higher than standard copper wires that companies lost confidence that they could compete in mass markets.

Although bismuth-based wires have been useful for research and in a few products that help stabilize power grids, the spotlight has shifted to another compound, a mixture of yttrium, barium, copper, and oxide generally called YBCO (pronounced IB-co).

YBCO tape cannot yet match bismuth's performance. But it used nickel instead of silver as a wire strengthener and "thin film" technology borrowed from the semiconductor and photovoltaic industries to deposit the layers of the tape, which then can be made into wire.

The technology will cut the cost of production up to 80 percent form the first-generation technology, said Dr. Yurek, whose company is the leading producer of the bismuth-based wire.

The last steps will not be easy. While the semiconductor industry works on improving technology to produce ever thinner films, superconductivity companies chase the opposite goal, making thicker films to carry more current.

The best available process for depositing YBCO involves blasting a chunk of it in a vacuum chamber with high-energy laser pulses and running the tape through the resulting plume. But pulsed lasers use too much time and money to produce large quantities of wire. So companies are looking for other methods.

"There's probably a dozen ways to deposit the superconductor," said Dr. Dean Peterson, head of the research program at the Los Alamos National Laboratory, which has been researching the alternatives and how to improve them.

As an added complication, technologies under development are competing to create the substrate under the superconducting ceramic. Although that material is less sexy, research indicates that the uniformity and alignment of the substrate are as crucial to obtaining useful wire as a foundation to a house.

As they race toward commercialization, the same question that attracted materials scientists to the field lurks in the background. Are better superconductors out there, waiting to be discovered?

Who hasn't played with a pair of magnets, trying to suspend one magnet above another? It seems impossible to keep a magnet suspended in this way as the upper magnet always falls at the slightest disturbance, shattering our dreams of simple magnetic levitation. However, using diamagnetic materials, which repel permanent magnets, the instability causing the collapse of magnetic levitation can be overcome. Ronald E. Pelrine, a senior research engineer at SRI International, an independent, nonprofit research institute, explains how carefully arranging diamagnetic materials can support objects in a stable fashion. With this kind of levitation, many applications, such as frictionless transport systems, become possible. —LCK

From "Diamagnetic Levitation"
by Ronald E. Pelrine
American Scientist, September/October 2004

The ability of magnets to exert forces on one another without touching intrigues most children and more than a few adults. It is a short step from pondering this curious phenomenon to wondering whether the force from one magnet could be used to levitate another, seemingly in defiance of gravity. Unfortunately, as any frustrated would be levitator has discovered, the answer is no: A magnetic field can be arranged so that at some position it just balances the gravitational force on a small magnet, but any disturbance to the levitated magnet, no matter how tiny, causes it to crash. This inherent lack of stability is summed up in a statement of physical law known as Earnshaw's Theorem, first elucidated in 1842. It is a direct consequence of Maxwell's fundamental equations describing electricity and magnetism.

Mastery of Maxwell's equations isn't needed to understand Earnshaw's Theorem. One needs merely to know that the behavior of a magnet can be described in terms of something called the magnetic potential, which is analogous to more familiar forms of potential energy (stored energy). Consider a marble placed on an undulating surface. The marble will roll in the direction that decreases its potential energy most rapidly, becoming free of any force only where the potential attains a local minimum—the flat bottom of a depression. Similarly, a levitated magnet would be stable only if it could be situated at a local minimum of the magnetic potential. But Maxwell's equations dictate that the magnetic potential at a point in space must be the average of the potential at surrounding positions. The magnetic potential thus cannot attain a local minimum anywhere in free space: Some nearby points will always have lower magnetic energy, while others will have higher energy.

Faced with the obvious implications of Earnshaw's Theorem, investigators have looked for other ways to levitate. The most common tactic is to use time-varying magnetic fields, to which Earnshaw's Theorem doesn't apply. Active-feedback levitation, for example, uses sensors to measure the position of a levitated object, adjusting the applied field in just the right way to keep things suspended. This approach has been used for decades in active magnetic bearings and experimental "maglev" trains. Although workable, such systems have considerable drawbacks: They consume power and are relatively complex, which means that they are expensive and can be prone to failure. But it turns out that there is a way to levitate a magnet without such complications. To understand how this feat can be carried out more simply, one needs at least a rudimentary understanding of the different types of magnetic materials.

The Right Stuff

Magnetic materials come in three flavors: ferromagnetic, paramagnetic, and diamagnetic. Ferromagnetic materials, such as iron, can often be permanently magnetized, allowing objects made of them, for example, to stick to refrigerator doors indefinitely. Paramagnetic substances, such as the mineral biotite, become magnetized only while they are exposed to an external magnetic field. They are attracted to permanent magnets and thus do not help in the quest for stable, passive levitation. Diamagnetic substances act differently. They repel permanent magnets, and in this way make such levitations rather easy.

A very simple model of the atom helps explain why diamagnetic materials act in this way. Consider an electron in orbit around the nucleus of an atom of diamagnetic material. Being a charge in motion, this electron generates a magnetic field that is just like that of a tiny current-carrying loop of wire. In the absence of an external magnetic field, this orbiting electron and its many neighbors generate randomly aligned fields, which cancel one another, so the material does not generate an overall field of its own. But when subjected to an external field (say, one from an approaching permanent magnet), these electrons speed up or slow down so as to oppose the change in the field inside their orbits. (This is just the atomic-scale version of a rule of electricity and magnetism called Lenz's Law.) The net effect is an induced magnetization that opposes the applied field, causing a repulsive force.

One can exploit this force to levitate permanent magnets above fixed diamagnetic materials. Or one can reverse things and levitate diamagnetic materials above one or more stationary magnets. The German physicist Werner Braunbeck demonstrated such diamagnetic levitation for the first time in 1939 when he floated some strongly diamagnetic materials (bismuth and graphite) using a fixed electromagnet. The stable levitation of small permanent magnets above superconductors, a familiar sight in recent years, is just another form of diamagnetic levitation: Superconductors are not only perfectly conductive, they are highly diamagnetic.

How is it that this form of levitation does not violate Earnshaw's Theorem? The answer is that the theorem applies only to a static magnetic field, and in such diamagnetic levitations the motion of the suspended magnet itself causes the levitating field to change. If, for example, a floating magnet is pushed downward, it induces a stronger repulsive field in the diamagnetic material below, lifting the magnet back up. Likewise, if some disturbance causes the suspended magnet to rise a bit, the supportive magnetic field diminishes, easing the payload back down. In a sense, the diamagnetic material automatically accomplishes what the sensors and electronic controls do in an active-feedback levitation system.

Surely such remarkable diamagnetic materials must have exotic compositions or be hard to fabricate, right? Not at all. Diamagnetic substances are everywhere. Indeed, in a basic sense, all materials are diamagnetic, but in ferromagnetic and paramagnetic objects this universal property is masked by stronger magnetic effects. Water, most plastics and glasses, and many ceramics and metals are diamagnetic. Bismuth is strongly diamagnetic, and a form of carbon known as pyrolytic graphite shows the highest diamagnetism of all at room temperature. It has this property because some of its electrons effectively travel in larger-than-normal orbits, so the magnetic field they produce from diamagnetism is much stronger than that generated in other materials. . .

Balancing Act

The fact that diamagnetic levitation can be stable does not mean it always will be stable. Proper design is needed. The basic idea in levitating diamagnetic materials is to set up a geometry that can support the object against gravity and at the same time ensure stability.

One straightforward approach is to arrange two like magnetic poles so that they face each other but are separated by a gap. The fields of the two magnetic poles thus cancel completely halfway between them. Poised at that one spot, a small piece of diamagnetic material has zero magnetic energy. Any deflection only increases its magnetic energy, which makes this midpoint a stable energy minimum. Although this configuration is conceptually simple to understand, it proves somewhat difficult to implement in practice.

Other geometries provide for the levitation of an anisotropic diamagnetic material (one in which the degree of diamagnetism depends on the direction of the applied field), such as pyrolytic graphite, which is typically formed using the decomposition of a high-temperature gas to deposit carbon atoms in a carefully controlled manner on a solid substrate. A horizontal slab of pyrolitic graphite is strongly repelled by vertical fields but is little affected by in-plane fields. So, for example, a flat graphic ring (one shaped like an ordinary washer) can readily be made to levitate above the junction between two concentric magnetic rings, where the field is horizontal. Interestingly, such a graphite ring is free to rotate as it floats. . .

The Magic of Levitation

Diamagnetic levitation is a striking physical phenomenon, one that has been studied for many decades now. Yet surprisingly few people, even scientists and engineers, are familiar with it. One reason is that, with the exception of some kits being sold as scientific novelties, diamagnetic levitation has not yet been exploited commercially—although various possibilities, including useful sensors and frictionless transport systems, have been fashioned in academic and industrial labs.

Why did so many decades pass between the first demonstration of diamagnetic levitation in 1939 and the development of useful devices based on this principle? The chief reason is that powerful neodymium-iron magnets, which make diamagnetic levitation quite easy today, were discovered only in the 1980s and didn't become widely available until the 1990s. In that sense, diamagnetic levitation was invented long before its time.

I first became familiar with this phenomenon in the mid-1980s during my Ph.D. studies, while trying to figure out how to design tiny robotic manipulators. The notion was that if these could be controlled to high precision at small scales, one could put together a compact system with all the mechanical complexity and precision of a modern manufacturing facility. Such a "microfactory" might be used, say, to mass-produce small-scale components at very low cost, to analyze compounds or for drug screening.

The engineering challenges to fashioning such a system are, of course, formidable. The biggest problem is that a centimeter-scale robot is extremely difficult to make autonomous, because it would need to carry on-board power, controls, navigation systems and so forth. The best way to overcome this obstacle, I realized, was to put the power and controls elsewhere and to exert magnetic or electrostatic forces on the robotic manipulators from external fixtures. Still, I needed to figure out what sort of bearings would allow the microrobots to move around. Conventional techniques just wouldn't do: Sliding surfaces have problems with friction and wear, and tiny wheels would be difficult to make and assemble.

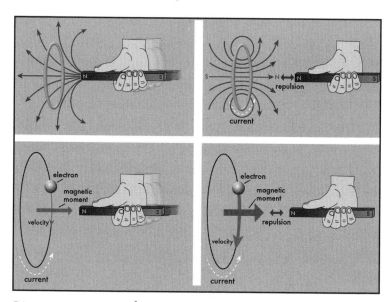

Diamagnetism arises from an atomic-scale version of Lenz's Law, which dictates that altering the magnetic flux through a conductive loop of wire *(upper left)* will induce electric currents that in turn give rise to a magnetic field opposing the change *(upper right)*. In a diamagnetic material, an electron in orbit around an atom acts, in a sense, like a conductive loop of wire, speeding up or slowing down so as to oppose any change in the magnetic field it experiences *(bottom)*. The magnetization induced in a diamagnetic object thus always manifests itself as a repulsive force.

Levitation seemed the natural solution. But imagine the difficulty of actively levitating, say, 1,000 micro-robots, particularly if they needed to interact. The failure of even one sensor or control circuit could cause havoc. I thus began to investigate diamagnetic levitation, which, being automatic and virtually 100 percent reliable, might make the envisioned system of interacting micro-robots feasible . . .

... Were they ever to be applied in outer space, diamagnetic forces might prove quite useful there as well. The absence of gravity would allow large gaps between the levitated object and the rest of the apparatus. One can imagine such arrangements being used for vibration isolation or to support flywheels, which are commonly employed in spacecraft to store angular momentum. Diamagnetic forces might also provide a convenient way for astronauts to manipulate objects without making physical contact with them.

Indeed, applying diamagnetic levitation in space gets around its one major disadvantage here on Earth: The bearing pressure that can currently be obtained is too low for most mechanical applications. However, there is no fundamental reason why the diamagnetism of specially designed materials could not be 10 or even 100 times greater than what's available now. If such substances could be identified and developed, diamagnetic levitation would be instantly catapulted from a little-known curiosity to a major technology. Transportation engineers might, for example, consider building maglev trains in this way.

Barring such a breakthrough, diamagnetic levitation will still surely find practical use through incremental improvements in magnets, materials, and designs. In any case, diamagnetic levitation is a fascinating physical phenomenon worthy of continued study. It incorporates a rich mix of electromagnetic theory, materials science, and engineering design to achieve systems with unusual properties and a truly

magical feel. I'm confident that future work in this area
will yield some intriguing surprises.

Reprinted with permission from *American Scientist*, © 2004, Written by Ronald E. Pelrine

*A plasma, a collection of positive and negative
charges that are not bound together as atoms, is
often called the fourth state of matter, the state
that is reached after heating a solid through its
liquid and gaseous states. In the quest for a
clean energy source, physicists work with fusion
plasmas at 100 million degrees, and in those
conditions, charged microparticles can collect
into a "dusty plasma." But as Robert Merlino
and John Goree, professors of physics at the
University of Iowa in Iowa City, explain, a dusty
plasma in a laboratory or studied in space can
be a source of interesting physics. —LCK*

From "Dusty Plasmas in the Laboratory, Industry, and Space"
by Robert L. Merlino and John A. Goree
Physics Today, July 2004

What do the rings of Saturn have in common with
industrial reactors used to manufacture semiconductor
microchips? Both are examples of systems containing
charged dust particles whose dynamics are controlled

by electromagnetic and gravitational forces. More specifically, they are examples of dusty plasmas, defined as partially or fully-ionized gases that contain micron-size particles of electrically charged solid material, either dielectric or conducting. Dusty plasmas are common in astrophysical environments; examples range from the interstellar medium to cometary tails and planetary ring systems.

The role of dust in cosmic and laboratory plasmas was discussed early on by Irving Langmuir, Lyman Spitzer, and Hannes Alfvén, three pioneers of plasma physics in the 20th century.[1] In a 1924 speech, Langmuir described the "profound effects" he observed in an arc discharge when minute droplets of tungsten vapor were sputtered from the cathode into the plasma. He ascribed the unusual effects to the attachment of electrons to the droplets, causing them to become negatively charged and thus move about under the influence of the electric fields within the discharge. It seems clear that Langmuir was describing the first laboratory observation of a dusty plasma.

Spitzer, in 1941, first discussed the processes by which dust particles in the interstellar medium acquire charge. He pointed out that, in addition to photoelectric charging by UV radiation, the dust particles acquire a negative charge due to their immersion in an ionized gas, even though the system's net charge is zero. The dust particles become negatively charged simply because their encounters with the swift electrons are more frequent than with the lumbering ions. Alfvén, in his 1954 monograph *On the Origin of the Solar System*, considered how the coagulation of dust particles in the solar nebula could have led to planetesimals and subsequently to comets and planets.

Watershed Events

Over the past 20 years, the publication rate on the subject of dusty plasmas has grown exponentially, spurred by two watershed discoveries. The first occurred in the early 1980s. Images of Saturn's rings taken by *Voyager 2* revealed certain features in the B ring that were probably as mysterious to modern planetary scientists as the rings themselves were to Galileo in 1610. The *Voyager* images (see figure 1, page 149) revealed a pattern of nearly radial "spokes" rotating around the outer portion of Saturn's dense B ring.[2] As the spacecraft approached the planet, the spokes first appeared dark against the bright background. But as *Voyager 2* withdrew from the Saturnian system, the spokes appeared brighter than the material around them.

This observation—that the spoke material scatters sunlight more effectively in the forward direction—indicated that the material is a fine dust. Perhaps the most interesting aspect of the discovery of the spokes was that they are not stationary structures. Indeed, they develop remarkably fast, with new spokes forming in as little as five minutes. This short dynamical time scale rules out explanations based solely on gravitational effects, indicating that the dust particles are affected by electromagnetic fields.

The first proposals that the spokes might consist of charged dust came from Jay Hill and Asoka Mendis at the University of California, San Diego, and independently from Christoph Goertz and Greg Morfill in

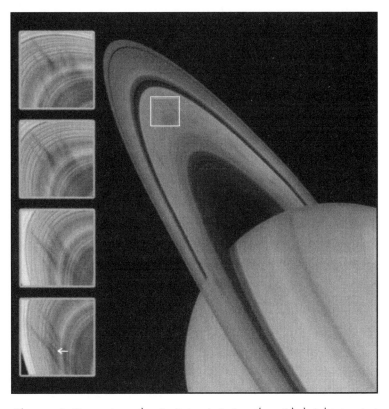

Figure 1. Dynamic spokes in Saturn's B ring, the wide bright ring just inside the prominent dark Cassini ring. The square fields at left are successive detailed images of the same orbiting physical region (light-colored square), taken at roughly 10-minute intervals by *Voyager 2* in 1981. The observed pattern of nearly radial "spokes," appearing dark against a bright background as the spacecraft approaches from the Sun side, changes quite rapidly. New spokes form in as little as five minutes, which suggests that the fine dust particles that compose them are affected by electromagnetic fields. *(Courtesy Calvin J. Hamilton)*

Germany.[3] Goertz and Morfill showed that the charged dust particles were electrostatically levitated about 80 km above the ring plane. They attributed the charging to bursts of plasma generated in localized regions by micrometeoroids that sporadically plunge into boulders in the rings.

The insertion of the *Cassini* spacecraft into orbit around Saturn as this issue of *Physics Today* goes to press should provide the dusty-plasma community with another boost of exciting results. Cameras aboard *Cassini*, with higher spatial and temporal resolution than *Voyager*'s, will give us a much-improved view of the formation and evolution of the spokes.

The second crucial development in dusty-plasma research, in the late 1980s, expanded the field across disciplinary boundaries. Scientists in the semiconductor industry, rather than astrophysicists, stumbled onto a significant discovery as they searched for the source of particulate contamination of semiconductor wafers. It had been widely believed that particle contamination of silicon substrates occurred mainly during handling of wafers in air. So attention was focused on improving clean-room standards. Nobody thought to check whether the contamination might be happening inside the plasma processing reactors that are used to deposit and etch thin films on the wafers.

But then Gary Selwyn of IBM made a serendipitous discovery. He was carrying out a routine measurement with laser-induced fluorescence, to determine the concentrations of reactive gases in a plasma.[4] When Selwyn shined his laser into the plasma, his attempted measurement of weak optical fluorescence was over-whelmed by scattering of the incident light. The laser light was illuminating clouds of micron-sized particles electrically suspended in the plasma above the wafer (see figure 2).

Selwyn found that particles actually formed and grew in the gas phase aggregating material from gases that were thought to have been exhausted by the vacuum

Figure 2. Rings of dust particles encircling silicon wafers in a plasma processing device. In an accidental 1989 discovery, laser light was shone into a plasma used to etch Si wafers so that the expected weak optical fluorescence would monitor concentrations of reactive gas. Instead, the fluorescence was overwhelmed by scattering of the incident light off unanticipated clouds of micron-sized particles electrically suspended in the plasma above the wafers.[4] Although great pains had been taken to minimize dust contamination of the clean room, it was discovered that the particles actually formed and grew in the plasma. When the RF power that generates the plasma is turned off, the particles fall onto the wafer, contaminating it. An electron-microscope image *(inset)* of a 20-μm-diameter particle from such a dust cloud. (Adapted from ref. 18.)

pump. Then, at the fateful moment when the plasma-generating RF power was switched off, the particles fell and contaminated the wafer. Selwyn's discovery revealed that much of the particle contamination responsible for costly yield losses was happening not just anywhere in the clean rooms, but inside the plasma reactors. . .

Dust in Fusion Plasmas

Much of plasma physics is devoted to developing controlled nuclear fusion. Igniting a fusion plasma requires heating deuterium and tritium nuclei to temperatures above 100 million kelvin. At such high temperatures, however, any solid material is vaporized and highly ionized. Therefore nobody expected that dust particles could exist in a fusion plasma, much less that they could be a source of concern.[5] It turns out, however, that a magnetically confined fusion plasma is in many ways dominated by the conditions at its edges, where it comes near material surfaces. The outer portions of the plasma typically have temperatures hundreds of times cooler than its center. In this more benign edge plasma, solid particles can survive briefly. Indeed, inspection of the bottoms of magnetic-confinement fusion devices after periods of operation shows the presence of fine dust particles.

The particles originate from the solid surfaces exposed to the plasma. Ion bombardment of the lining material (often graphite) liberates atoms that are thought to form dust particles and deposit thin films on other chamber surfaces. As semiconductor engineers know too well, such films easily flake off, creating dust particles that fall down. In a fusion energy reactor, the ion bombardment would be ferocious and long lasting, and the resulting accumulation of dust could be enormous. That poses safety issues because dust particles can retain hazardous quantities of radioactive tritium. . .

. . . Astrophysical and space plasmas are typically much less dense than laboratory plasmas. And they are subjected to much more UV light. Consequently, the dominant process for charging dust particles in astrophysical plasmas is often photoelectron emission rather than the collection of ambient electrons and ions. Photoelectric charging is apparently responsible for the seemingly bizarre reports of "Moon clouds" by Apollo astronauts in the 1960s and 70s. The report of a "weird glow" on the horizon of the Moon turned out to be the reflection of sunlight from Moon dust particles photoelectrically charged and electrostatically levitated above the lunar surface.[8] . . .

Redefining the Fourth State

Plasma is often termed "the fourth state of matter" because adding energy to a solid converts it first to a liquid, then to a gas, and finally to a plasma. With a dusty plasma, this progression closes into a circle. It is a plasma that can have the properties of a liquid or a solid. It forces us to reconsider exactly what is meant by the term plasma. Defining plasma as a collection of positive and negative charges that are not atomically bound to one another, we encounter two possibilities. Most commonly, the charges have abundant kinetic energy and fly easily past their neighbors, much like molecules in a gas. That's termed a weakly coupled plasma.

The obverse is the less common strongly coupled plasma, which has charged particles whose kinetic energy is much less than the electrostatic potential energy between neighbors. Previously, the best-known strongly coupled plasmas included the interiors of stars and laser-cooled ion aggregates. In stellar interiors, the ratio γ of electrostatic to kinetic energy is large because of high density and small interparticle spacing. . .

. . . Box 2 also shows an example of the diagnostic techniques that have been developed not only to image static patterns of dust particles in a plasma but also to permit a complete mapping of their individual motions in dynamical situations.[12] Nothing like that can be done for the ions of ordinary plasmas, for which one can only measure statistical distributions. The ability to image dusty plasmas at the particle level lets researchers study the melting phase transition, phonons, and other condensed matter phenomena with unprecedented directness.[13]

One manifestation of phonons that is uncommon in molecular solids is the so-called Mach cone, a V-shaped wake created by a moving supersonic disturbance. In a laboratory dusty plasma, Mach cones are made by applying force to the particles by means of laser light. Using a setup like that shown in box 2, one of us (Goree) and coworkers swept an argon laser beam across a monolayer suspension of plastic microparticles.[12] The laser sweep caused a moving disturbance. The microparticles were illuminated for imaging by light from a much weaker helium-neon laser. . .

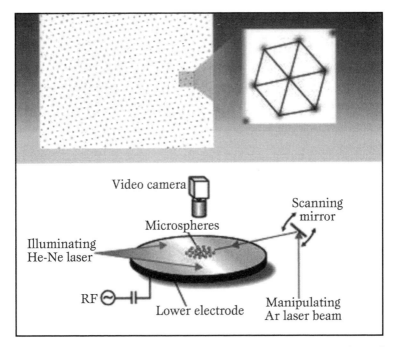

Box 2: Formation of a Coulomb Crystal. In a number of experiments, one of us (Goree) and coworkers formed plasmas by applying RF power to the 23-cm-diameter electrode at the bottom of a parallel-plate plasma chamber. From a "salt shaker" above the electrode, we sprinkled 8-μm-diameter plastic spheres into the plasma. The particles acquire negative charge by collecting electrons from the plasma. Thus they become levitated as a horizontal mono-layer several millimeters above the lower electrode. The suspended microparticles organize themselves by mutual electrostatic repulsion into a planar triangular Coulomb lattice with hexagonal symmetry.[11] The pattern is illuminated by a sheet of helium-neon laser light and imaged by a video camera. For more dynamical studies, we can dis-turb the microparticles with an intense, steerable argon laser beam. (*Courtesy of* Physics Today *and the American Institute of Physics*)

Microgravity Experiments

The weightlessness provided by space vehicles in orbital free fall is ideal for experiments on dusty plasmas. On the ground, experimenters must contend with gravity. The prospect of a weightless laboratory environment was so attractive that the first physics experiment on the *International Space Station* (ISS), begun in February 2001, was a dusty-plasma experiment.[15]

The experiment is a German-Russian collaboration. The plasma chamber, built in Germany for the space station, has been named the Nefedov Plasma Crystal Experiment in honor of Anatoli Nefedov, a leader of the Russian contingent who died in 2001. The apparatus, similar to the one shown in box 2, is about the size of a microwave oven. A video image of one of the dust structures (figure 5) shows a variety of features, including a sharply defined void in the center, a stable crystal-like array below the void, and fluid vortices along the horizontal axis and outer edges.

In the absence of gravity, one has the opportunity to see both liquid- and solidlike phenomena as other forces emerge to affect the dynamics of the dust. Charged dust particles in plasma are affected by their mutual electro-static interaction and by interaction with gas molecules and ions. Thermal gradients produce thermophoretic forces. Ion drag, which can be the dominant force under weightless conditions, is thought to have caused the void seen in figure 5 by pushing dust particles out of the center of the plasma chamber's RF discharge. . .

The imposing intellectual range of physics issues touched on by the study of dusty plasmas extends beyond plasma physics to include, for example, the solid-liquid melting transition and vortex flows in fluids. And size range of dusty-plasma applications extends

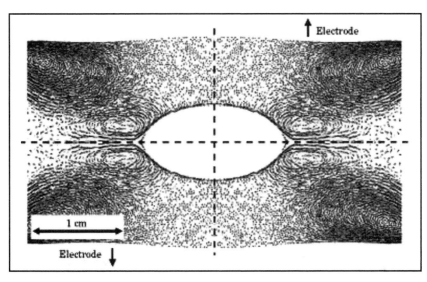

Figure 5. A weightless dusty plasma in the Nefedov Plasma Crystal Experiment aboard the *International Space Station*, an RF-powered plasma discharge chamber device similar to that shown in box 2. The single-frame video image shows that, in the weightless space station environment, the micron-size dust particles fill the entire three-dimensional plasma volume except for a well-defined central void from which dust particles are expelled by ions retreating from a region of positive plasma potential. The dust distribution exhibits fluid-like vortices as well as stable crystal-like domains.

from microgrooves in semiconductor devices to the magisterial rings of Saturn.

References:

1. I. Langmuir, C. G. Found, A. F. Dittmer, *Science* **60**, 392 (1924); Alfvén, *On the Origin of the Solar System*, Clarendon Press, Oxford, UK (1954); L. Spitzer Jr, *Physical Processes in the Interstellar Medium*, Wiley, New York (1978).
2. B. A. Smith *et al., Science* **215**, 504 (1982) [INSPEC].
3. C. J. Hill, D. A. Mendis, *Moon and Planets*, **23**, 53 (1980) [INSPEC]; C. K. Goertz, G. Morfill, *Icarus* **53**, 219 (1983) [INSPEC]; C. K. Goertz, *Rev. Geophys.* **27**, 271 (1989) [INSPEC]; M. Horanyi, *Annu. Rev. Astron. Astrophys.* **34**, 383 (1996) [CAS].
4. G. S. Selwyn, J. Singh, R. S. Bennett, *J. Vac. Sci. Technol.* **A7**, 2758 (1989).

5. J. Winter, *Phys. Plasmas* **7**, 3862 (2000) [INSPEC]; K. Narihara *et al., Nucl. Fusion* **37**, 1177 (1997) [INSPEC]; S. I. Krasheninnikov, Y. Tomita, R. D. Smirnov, K. K. Janev, *Phys. Plasmas* **11**, 3141 (2004) [SPIN].

8. See http://www.space.com/scienceastronomy/top_10_weird.html.

12. A. Melzer, S. Nunomura, D. Samsonov, Z. W. Ma, J. Goree, *Phys. Rev. E.* **62**, 4162 (2000) [INSPEC].

13. A. Melzer, A. Homann, A. Piel, *Phys. Rev. E.* **53**, 2757 (1996) [INSPEC]; H. M. Thomas, G. Morfill, *J. Vac. Sci. Technol.* **14**, 501 (1996) [SPIN].

15. A. Nefedov *et al., New J Phys.* **5**, 33.1 (2003).

Reprinted with permission from American Institute of Physics, © 2004, Written by Robert L. Merlino and John A. Goree, Fig. 1, Calvin J. Hamilton, Fig. 2, Adapted from G. S. Selwyn, *Plasma Sources Science Technology*, Box 2 and Fig. 4, Reprinted with permission from *Physics Today* and American Institute of Physics, © 2004, Fig. 5, Adapted from A. Nefedov *et al. New Journal of Physics*

Gravitational Force on a Human Scale

5

It may surprise anyone who has a perfectly spherical globe representing our home, Earth, to learn that our planet isn't a perfect sphere. And it isn't a perfect oblate spheroid either. It's lumpy, with great chunks of dense materials poking out above the surface. Not only that, the lumpiness moves about; the mantle underneath the crust of Earth is continuously moving, the masses of ice locked up in the poles and in glaciers expand or melt, and water levels in the oceans rise or fall. Understanding these changing conditions is an important task of scientists as they monitor our global weather system, for example. Recently, two satellites were launched with the purpose of measuring changes in Earth's structure, by measuring minute changes in Earth's gravitational pull. At any point above Earth's surface, the gravitational force of Earth depends on the local mass and, hence, depends on the distribution of Earth's lumpiness. Writer Warren E. Leary reports on how the pair of satellites will use the global positioning system

*to make fine detailed measurements of the
gravitational force.* —*LCK*

"New Satellites to Map Gravity"
by Warren E. Leary
New York Times, March 19, 2002

No one thinks that much about gravity, one of the most powerful, yet subtle, forces on the earth. It is just there, seemingly never changing, holding feet to the ground.

Now scientists say it is time for a new look at gravity. Minute variations around the globe, they say, can tell us about the earth and what's going on beneath the surface of the land and the oceans, where dynamic processes are constantly moving around masses of material.

To get the most detailed measurements ever taken of these changes, scientists have launched the Gravity Recovery and Climate Experiment, or Grace.

The project, sponsored by the National Aeronautics and Space Administration and the German Aerospace Center (or DLR), consists of a pair of satellites nick-named Tom and Jerry, which will follow and monitor each other in space and, in the process, produce a gravity map of the planet 100 times as accurate and detailed as any done before.

"The Grace measurements are going to revolutionize our understanding of the earth's structure, the oceans and the changes going on underneath," said Dr. Michael Watkins, project scientist at NASA's Jet Propulsion Laboratory. "Measuring gravitational variations gives us a window for watching the transport of masses around the planet, changes that can affect climate and many other things."

Gravity measurements can be used to track the movement and changing density of ice at the poles, the transport of huge volumes of water in deep undersea currents, the movement of water in and out of underground aquifers and even the slow shift of magma in volcanically active regions, Dr. Watkins said. As scientists refine the Grace data, they hope to measure snowfall and how much water it contains.

The satellites were launched on Sunday from the Plesetsk Cosmodrome in Russia using a single rocket supplied by Eurockot Launch Services, a German-Russian commercial launching company.

Both 950-pound satellites are to fly in the same 311-mile-high circular orbit that crosses the poles of the planet, as it turns beneath them during their 16 orbits each day. More important, one satellite is to trail the other by 137 miles, each using microwave range finders to measure the precise distance between the two, which is the key to the experiment. Sir Isaac Newton formulated the basic law of gravity in the 17th century. All objects, he said, attract one another with a force that is proportional to their masses and that is dependent upon the distances between them. Although the force of gravity is relatively constant everywhere on earth, small variations exist because the planet is not a homogeneous structure with equally distributed mass. The planet is lumpy, with materials of different densities scattered above and below the surfaces of land and water. "Gravity varies," said Dr. Byron D. Tapley, director of the Center for

Space Research at the University of Texas and the principal investigator in charge of Grace. "Gravity is less on a mountaintop than at the seashore." Previous gravity maps of earth have been created by using gravitational fluctuations that affect a single satellite, or by combining ground-tracking data on the orbits of several spacecraft. But these imprecise snapshots of the planet's gravity are no longer adequate, scientists say. "Before, scientists wanted to measure gravity one time, and be done with it,'" Dr. Tapley said. "Now we realize that gravity is not constant and is continually changing."

Grace is to produce a gravity map of earth's entire surface every 30 days; during its five-year service, it should produce 60 maps, showing subtle changes over time. "It's this temporal element that will make the data so valuable," Dr. Tapley said. The Grace measurements should be very exacting because each satellite should track the other with extreme precision. The trapezoidal-shaped spacecraft are equipped with Global Positioning System receivers that use information from the navigational tool to pinpoint its position relative to the other and to the ground. The satellites also contain highly sensitive sensors, called accelerometers. These detect changes in motion caused by atmospheric drag or even by sunlight hitting its solar power panels, thus allowing scientists to cancel the effects of these forces as they make their measurements. The satellites' microwave range finders will constantly measure the distance between them to sense any change in separation greater than one micron—about one-fiftieth the width of a human hair. "This is like measuring the precise distance between a car in Los Angeles and one in San Diego to within the thickness of a particle of smoke," Dr. Watkins said. Variations in distance caused by gravity difference on earth produce data points for the gravity map.

As the satellites move in their orbit, the first one senses a mass change caused by a mountain, glacier, or swell of water in a deep ocean current. This mass pulls the first satellite a little toward it before it tugs the second spacecraft, slightly changing the separation between the two. After the first satellite passes an object below, it slows down slightly (because of the attraction), before the trailing spacecraft is similarly affected, again registering a slight change in distance between the two. These fine pulls and tugs on the spacecraft slowly sketch out a map of the masses below.

Researchers said data from the $127 million mission—$97 million coming from NASA and $30 million, including launching costs, from Germany—would initially benefit ocean and climate research. Information from other spacecraft using radar or laser scanning to measure sea height, like the Topex/Poseidon satellite, can be combined with the gravity data to obtain better estimates of sea-surface temperatures that affect weather. For instance, if researchers notice a rise in water levels in the Pacific Ocean, it can be from heat expanding the water, a sign of future El Nino conditions. The water level rise, however, may also be because of winds deforming the ocean surface and pushing up a mass of water, a condition that Grace could spot. This additional data, therefore, can help improve the accuracy of weather and climate forecasting, scientists said.

Tracing the gravity signature of moving masses can also help monitor the movement and changing size of polar ice, which is affected by global warming. "You can determine, for example, if the sea level is rising because there is actually more water melting into it or if the water is expanding simply due to heating," Dr. Watkins said.

Subtle gravity differences can also provide information about the structure of earth's interior, including the tectonic processes that continue to reshape the surface and move continents. Previous orbital studies have revealed an area of lower-than-normal gravity off the coasts of India, as well as a gravity-high area in the South Pacific, both possibly due to the structure of mantle material beneath the crust.

There is a commonly held myth that when you are out in space, gravity releases its hold on you and you become weightless. The truth is, the only time you can be completely weightless is when you are in free fall or in orbit around an astronomical object such as a planet. Gravity's reach extends far into space above Earth's surface. If you were to stand on a ladder that reached as far as the orbit of the space shuttle, your weight would only drop a mere 10 percent. So why do the images of the astronauts

in the space shuttle show them floating around weightless? The trick is that orbit is just another way of going into free fall, a free fall trajectory that continuously misses Earth and so never reaches the ground. The astronauts experience weightlessness the same way someone jumping out of an airplane does in the seconds before his or her parachute opens.

In fact, the weightless environment is routinely achieved at much lower altitudes than the space shuttle's orbital height. In this article, science writer John Schwartz describes the experiences of science students aboard the NASA KC-135 Low Gravity Plane, a jet that cycles through steep parabolic flight paths to give people the experience of, and allow for experiments to be conducted in, a gravity-free environment. This plane, also known as the Vomit Comet, is used to train astronauts and test space technology. —LCK

"Free from Gravity, These Students Taste Outer Space"
by John Schwartz
New York Times, June 8, 2004

On the ceiling of the NASA KC-135 low-gravity plane, over the Gulf of Mexico—"Feet down!" Normally, those words are a description of the world as we know it. Feet down. Head up. Horizon level. But up here, where gravity is briefly defeated dozens of times an hour as this jet cycles through up-and-down parabolas 10,000 feet high, it is a command, and a warning. It says that the period of weightlessness is ending, that gravity is about to return with a vengeance as the plane swings up and that the passengers need to be in position for a soft landing on the plane's padded floor. Such is life aboard KC-135, the four-engine military version of the Boeing 707 that the National Aeronautics and Space Administration uses to train astronauts for weight-lessness, to test in-space technology, to help Hollywood shoot weightless scenes—and to let dozens of engineering students each year know that the space program might be a cool place to work.

"You are really the hope for the future of this country," Gregory W. Hayes, director of external relations for the Johnson Space Center, said to several teams of college students who had traveled to Houston for a one-week program that culminates in their conducting experiments aboard the microgravity plane.

Mr. Hayes's pitch was urgent. America's pipeline in science and engineering is drying up at a time the nation is in desperate need of innovation. The year-over-year increase in the number of engineering graduates that China is turning out, he said, is greater than the total number of engineers who are graduating from American schools. "Frankly," he told them, "the statistics are alarming." Once the "industry of choice" for tech-nical workers, aerospace now "presents a negative image to potential employees" because of years of cutbacks, consolidation and stagnation, a recent study by the Aerospace Industries Association found. Top students with scientific or technological bents are more likely to choose hot fields like biotechnology. NASA, after all, does not grant stock options.

At the same time, NASA's brains and hands are aging. Partly because of longstanding hiring freezes that are just beginning to thaw, NASA employees older than 60 outnumber those younger than 30 by three to one, according to the General Accounting Office.

The plans to return to the Moon and push on to Mars make it even more imperative to attract young engineers, NASA officials say. "It's all going to happen in your career time," an astronaut, Dr. Bonnie J. Dunbar, told the students.

That is why NASA is looking more than ever to educational initiatives like the student flight program, in which college students devise and build experiments that can be performed aboard the KC-135, also known as the K-Bird.

Steven H. Collicott, a professor of engineering at Purdue, said the program, which began in 1996, is like "a high school science fair on steroids."

The plane has another nickname, from its reputation for causing nausea in some fliers. They call it the Vomit Comet. NASA has made great strides in controlling the symptoms, and scientists say they still cannot predict who will be sick and who will not. But they nevertheless distribute a government-issue motion-sickness bag to each flier, along with a lecture on "bag etiquette."

"I am so-o going to be the one who loses his lunch!" Brian Ventre, a big, sardonic engineer from Purdue said on the first day of the visit in April. "I won't," Rebecca Karnes, another member of the team, said. "I'm determined." The Purdue project is to develop and test a new pipe that can be deployed in space, perhaps as a conduit for wires or a boom for antennas. The students have worked far into many nights on the pipe, two pieces of thin flexible Kevlar strips shaped like rounded metal measuring tape and glued together to leave an eye-shape space in the middle. The two curved pieces can be flattened together and rolled tightly around a reel for storage before flight. In space, astronauts would play out the boom, which would pop back to its original shape and stiffen. The experiment itself is homely and has a hand-built look, not to mention its mascot, Bob, a pink plastic flamingo with Mardi Gras beads, attached to the experiment's frame with duct tape. The team T-shirt is gray with an embroidered flamingo. The students maintain a Web site with a running account of their progress at www.livejournal.com/users/purduezerog/.

NASA is eager to have them do everything they can to share the experience, including taking a reporter along with the team. The point, NASA officials say, is to spread the word about the space program to people who do not have an opportunity to ride the plane. Next to them in the hangar at Ellington Airfield in Houston is a team from the University of San Diego, a Roman Catholic institution in California. That team's experiment is a refrigerator-size machine that shakes racks of differently shaped containers, each filled with small beads and one larger one. The idea is to test out a physics question known as the Brazil nut problem. That problem asks why in a can of mixed nuts do the Brazil nuts almost always work their way to the top? Understanding the physics of how objects shake out in low gravity could help determine how to pack objects collected on the surfaces of the Moon or on Mars.

The experiment itself is so sleek that it could have been designed by Porsche, the acrylic containers precision-shaped by a contractor and the heavy-motor shaking mechanism smooth and powerful. The team itself arrived in matching blue flight suits with their names at the breast pockets. In the movie version, the experiments would be a geeky version of the soapbox derby competitions. The Purdue team would be the scrappy upstart kids, and the San Diego crew would be the snooty rich kids with their Daddy-built roadsters. But this is not a competition. The rivalries are friendly. Everybody has one goal, and that is to board the plane.

That first day, another astronaut, Dr. Daniel T. Barry, told the students that the microgravity experience aboard the plane was "exactly like being in space." This is not just a pep talk. The sensation of weightlessness aboard the space shuttle and International Space Station is actually free fall, just like the 30-second drops the students will experience. The spacecraft are constantly falling toward Earth, their altitude maintained by their orbital speed. Dr. Barry offered this advice: "You don't want to get too wrapped up in the experiments" and miss the experience of weightlessness. "Remember. Very few people are going to ask you how the experiment went. Everybody is going to ask you what it was like [to be weightless]."

The students all understand that the experiments may not produce the results they are looking for, or even function at all. The San Diego crew's motor controller burned out two weeks before the flight and had to be replaced. The Purdue team's motor turned out to be too puny to roll and unroll the flattened boom. They had to create a hand crank on the fly, so to speak.

Not everyone is a fan of the K-Bird program. Dr. Charles M. Swenson, a professor of engineering at Utah State University, argues that it is showy, but does not do much to address the need to build the ranks of the nation's engineers. Other initiatives reach more students at a more impressionable age, Professor Swenson said. He offered as an example the Hitchhiker program, which allows students to put their own experiments on the space shuttle.

The programs he favors are being scaled back to carve billions from the NASA budget for President Bush's plan to send astronauts to the Moon and Mars. The microgravity flight program has also been trimmed from time to time, though the space agency insists that it is safe for now.

"I'm thinking it's looking pretty bleak," Professor Swenson said. As a recruiting tool for college engineering students, the flights can be powerful. "I would love to do something for NASA after college," said Adrianna Zammit, a second-time flier on the San Diego team. "I don't want to be in a cube for 40 hours a week for the rest of my life." Another student was not as impressed. Speaking without attribution for fear of offending the hosts, the student said, "I would not be interested in working at NASA," and argued that its human space flight efforts seemed overly bureaucratic. NASA scheduled two flights a day over the next week, with several groups on each.

The students are not the only ones who deal with uncertainty. On the Friday before the flights, one of the four engines on the KC-135 failed on a flight. NASA grounded it to replace the engine, delaying the schedule a day.

On Purdue's flight day, heartbreak. An engine light for the replaced engine went on, and the plane returned to Ellington after a third of its planned parabolas. The group pack edits work into the two sessions. The disappointment was palpable.

The next day, San Diego flew. Ms. Zammit said that the floating sensation gave her a feeling of freedom, but also that "having little control resulted in some feelings of anxiety." "The slightest push off the wall sent me flying across the plane cabin," she said.

On the last two parabolas, NASA gave the engineers in training a taste of what it would be like to walk on the Moon and Mars, adjusting the descent to simulate their gravitational pulls. The lunar gravity, one-sixth that of Earth, put a bounce in everyone's step that explains the jerky hoppiness of the Apollo-era video clips. Some students dropped down for one-finger pushups. Martian gravity, one-third that of Earth, is less bouncy but still gloriously weird. And then it was over.

"Ladies and gentlemen, that's a wrap!" John Yaniec, the flight director, announced. Despite the predictably unpredictable glitches, the students all captured their data for later review. Just one person, a Houston flight controller along for the ride, became ill. The controller, Colin Asekun, showed excellent etiquette. "Somebody had to keep the name Vomit Comet alive, right?" he said.

Gravity is described by Isaac Newton's central inverse-square force law, as far as is known, for all length scales from the microscopic to the astronomical. Gravity is also the weakest of all the fundamental forces, being many orders of magnitude smaller by comparison to the electromagnetic, strong, and weak forces. This has puzzled physicists, since there did not seem to be any good reason for this to be the case. Recently, however, new theories have made suggestions for the cause of gravity's weakness, spurring experiments that explore the validity of Newton's gravitational force law on very small scales.

Jonathan L. Feng, a physicist at the department of physics at the University of California at Irvine, has written a short article describing how the new theories add extra dimensions to our universe. He also describes how these extra dimensions, and deviations from Newtonian gravity, are being searched for in experiments on tabletops and in the explosive evaporations of short-lived black holes in our own atmosphere. —LCK

From "Searching for Gravity's Hidden Strength"
by Jonathan L. Feng
Science, **October 31, 2003**

Of the four known fundamental forces—gravity, electromagnetism, and the weak and strong forces—gravity is by far the weakest. The reasons for this weakness have long remained enigmatic. Recent proposals suggest, however, that the weakness of gravity may be evidence for extra spatial dimensions. Experiments ranging from tabletop tests of Newtonian gravity to searches for microscopic black holes in kilometer-scale detectors are now putting these ideas to the test.

The importance of gravity in everyday life results not from its strength but from its universality: Objects cannot be gravitationally neutral, and all bodies with mass attract. Yet as an interaction between elementary particles, gravity is extremely weak. For example, the gravitational attraction between two protons is 35 orders of magnitude weaker than their electromagnetic repulsion. This holds for protons separated by any distance r, because both gravitational and electromagnetic forces are proportional to $1/r^2$.

The observed weakness of gravity may, however, not be an intrinsic property of gravity, but may instead be an effect of extra spatial dimensions. This possibility is based on a simple consideration.

Suppose that our three-dimensional (3D) world is merely a subspace of a higher-dimensional space, and that gravity propagates freely in all dimensions, but that all other forces are confined to our three dimensions. In contrast to the familiar three dimensions, the extra dimensions are curled up in small circles of circumference L. Hence, moving a distance L in the direction of any of the extra dimensions brings one back to one's starting place.

Now suppose that at some separation distance $r < L$, gravity is strong, that is, comparable to electromagnetism. As r increases, the electromagnetic force drops as $1/r^2$. However, the gravitational field spreads out in all available spatial dimensions, and the gravitational force therefore decreases much more rapidly as $1/r^2 + n$, where n is the number of extra dimensions. This rapid drop continues until $r > L$, at which point the extra dimensions become less and less important and gravity recovers its $1/r^2$ behavior. . .

. . . [G]ravity is not intrinsically weak: It is as strong as electromagnetism at small length scales. It appears weak at the relatively large distances of common experience only because its effects are diluted by propagation in extra dimensions. The distance at which the gravitational and electromagnetic forces might have equal strength is unknown, but a particularly interesting possibility is that it is 10^{-19} m, the distance at which the electromagnetic and weak forces are known to unify to form the electroweak force.[1]

A priori, the size of the extra dimensions L and their number n are independent parameters. However, to achieve equality of gravitation and electromagnetic forces at 10^{-19} m, they become constrained by the relation $L = 10^{(32/n)-19}$ m (1).

For large n, the strength of gravity grows very rapidly at microscopic length scales. Gravity may then deviate from its $1/r^2$ behavior only at very small distances and still be comparable to electromagnetism at 10^{-19} m.

This scenario, called "large extra dimensions" because the length L of Eq. 1 is large relative to typical length scales in particle physics, raises many more questions than it answers. When first proposed, perhaps its most surprising aspect was that such a bold modification of Newtonian gravity was not immediately excluded by data. Now, however, a wide variety of experiments are reaching the sensitivity required to test these speculative ideas. In combination, they probe all possible values for the number of extra dimensions, placing the entire scenario on the threshold of detailed investigation.

The possibility of one large extra dimension is untenable. It requires the extra dimension to be of size $L = 10^{13}$ m, a length scale where the $1/r^2$ gravitational force law is clearly still valid. For two extra dimensions, each extra dimension would have L 1 mm. Sensitive tests of gravity are notoriously difficult at such length scales. Nonetheless, recent tabletop experiments with torsion pendulums have excluded significant deviations from the $1/r^2$ force law at length scales as small as 0.1 mm.[2]

Astrophysical observations provide less direct but more stringent constraints on low numbers of extra dimensions.[3, 4] For two extra dimensions, for example, the gravitational force would be enhanced at large enough length scales that supernovae should release much of their energy as gravitational energy—in conflict with observations. These constraints, which were noted immediately after the proposal of large extra dimensions, exclude scenarios with few extra dimensions.

The challenge, then, has been to explore large numbers of extra dimensions, such as the six or seven favored by string theory. In such cases, tabletop and astrophysical constraints are ineffective, because the predicted deviations from Newtonian gravity occur on length scales far below those that are currently accessible. The most promising approach is to look not for small effects at relatively large length scales, but for large effects at the smallest possible length scales, where gravity is predicted to be strong. These probes are equally powerful for any n. For low n, they are superseded by those discussed above, but for large n, they provide the leading experimental tests.

Perhaps the most remarkable possibility for testing large n has been the realization that if gravity is strong at 10^{-19} m, tiny black holes may form in high-energy particle collisions.[5-8] The formation of a black hole is expected when a large mass or, equivalently, a large energy is concentrated in a small volume.[9, 10] In the conventional 3D world, gravity is so weak that the required energy density is never achieved in observable particle collisions. However, if large extra dimensions exist and gravity is intrinsically strong, very high energy particles occasionally pass close enough to each other to trigger gravitational collapse, forming microscopic black holes. Like conventional black holes, these black holes are expected to emit "Hawking radiation," which leads to the evaporation of the black holes. In contrast to the astrophysical variety, however, they are tiny, with diameters on the order of 10^{-19} m, and evaporate explosively after only 10^{-27} s.

Today's particle colliders are not sufficiently energetic to produce microscopic black holes. However, ultrahigh-energy cosmic rays have been observed to collide with particles in Earth's atmosphere with center-of-mass energies that are 100 times those available at human-made colliders. The ultrahigh-energy neutrinos that are expected to accompany these cosmic rays may create microscopic black holes. Although these black holes are extremely short-lived and hence impossible to detect directly, their explosive evaporations produce events with unusual properties.[7, 8] The fact that no such events have been observed so far places strong constraints on large extra dimensions, but does not yet exclude these scenarios altogether.[11]

The search for large extra dimensions will intensify. The currently operating Antarctic Muon and Neutrino Detector Array and its successor IceCube are kilometer-scale cosmic neutrino detectors buried deep in the Antarctic ice. The Auger Observatory, consisting of water Cerenkov detectors covering a 3000-km^2 area in the high desert of Argentina, will also begin operation in 2 to 3 years. These large projects will provide enhanced sensitivity to the putative microscopic black holes.[12, 13] The Large Hadron Collider, currently under construction in Geneva, will provide an even higher sensitivity to large extra dimensions.

If no anomalous effects are seen in these ambitious projects, the possibility of large extra dimensions will be excluded. If seen and confirmed, however, these effects will provide the first evidence for strong gravity and a radically new view of spacetime.

References

1. N. Arkani-Hamed, S. Dimopoulos, G. R. Dvali, *Phys. Lett. B* **429**, 263 (1998) [ADS].
2. E. G. Adelberger *et al.*, http://arXiv.org/abs/hep-ex/0202008 (2002).
3. S. Cullen, M. Perelstein, *Phys. Rev. Lett.* **83**, 268 (1999) [APS].
4. L. J. Hall, D. R. Smith, *Phys. Rev. D* **60**, 085008 (1999) [APS].
5. S. B. Giddings, S. Thomas, *Phys. Rev. D* **65**, 056010 (2002) [APS].
6. S. Dimopoulos, G. Landsberg, *Phys. Rev. Lett.* **87**, 161602 (2001) [APS].
7. J. L. Feng, A. D. Shapere, *Phys. Rev. Lett.* **88**, 021303 (2001) [APS].
8. L. A. Anchordoqui, H. Goldberg, *Phys. Rev. D* **65**, 047502 (2002) [APS].
9. D. M. Eardley, S. B. Giddings, *Phys. Rev. D* **66**, 044011 (2002) [APS].
10. H. Yoshino, Y. Nambu, *Phys. Rev. D* **66**, 065004 (2002) [APS].
11. L. A. Anchordoqui et al., http://arXiv.org/abs/hep-ph/0307228 (2003).
12. M. Kowalski, A. Ringwald, H. Tu, *Phys. Lett. B* **529**, 1 (2002) [ADS].
13. J. Alvarez-Muniz *et al.*, *Phys. Rev. D* **65**, 124015 (2002) [APS].

Searching for Gravity's Hidden Strength, Reprinted with permission from AAAS, 302:795–797, Oct 31, 2003, written by Jonathan L. Feng

Gravity and Cosmology

6

Our everyday experience dictates that gravity is a distinct force that glues us, and the toast I just dropped, to the floor. So it may come as a surprise that gravity can be a wave when we take a look at how it is affected by massive astronomical bodies.

According to theories of general relativity, masses don't just generate a gravitational force, they curve the geometry of space and time together, which causes objects to fall in toward each other. And when large masses shift, such as when two black holes collide, ripples in the space-time geometry will radiate away as gravity waves.

In this excerpt, physicist Peter S. Shawhan, a staff scientist at the California Institute of Technology, explains some of the physics of gravity waves. He describes the development of a worldwide network of detectors designed to notice the minute changes in gravity due to cosmic events, helping scientists learn the true nature of gravity. —LCK

From "Gravitational Waves and the Effort to Detect Them"
by Peter S. Shawhan
American Scientist, July/August 2004

Somewhere out in space, two black holes may be colliding at this very moment, entwining their powerful gravitational fields in a death spiral that will culminate in a cataclysmic merger. Being black holes, they will emit no telltale x-ray burst, not even a flash of light, nothing at all to be seen by today's powerful telescopes. But the energy released by this violent event will radiate into the cosmos as ripples in the geometry of space and time.

An expanding group of investigators hopes eventually to detect the subtle gravitational echoes that reach the Earth from such dramatic astrophysical events. The signals are expected to be so minute that the apparatus needed to detect them must be capable of registering changes in length that are much smaller than the breadth of an atomic nucleus. Remarkably, this is now technologically feasible. Although substantial challenges remain in achieving the necessary sensitivities, the next few years should see the emergence of a worldwide network of instruments capable of measuring the gravitational radiation that astrophysicists are sure is out there waiting to be revealed.

Telling Space How to Curve

To understand how gravitational radiation arises and what sort of physical apparatus is needed to detect it requires at least a rudimentary understanding of

Einstein's general theory of relativity. This theory posits that time is a dimension similar to the three dimensions of space and that the combined four-dimensional "space-time" can be treated using the language of geometry.

The complete history of an object's position as a function of time is described by a "world line," which threads through the four-dimensional coordinate system, from past to present to future. If no force acts on the object, it will move with a constant velocity, and its world line will be a straight line at some fixed angle relative to the coordinate axes.

An object near a large mass feels the force of gravity accelerate it, so that its world line follows a curved path relative to the coordinate system. For example, if a ball is thrown straight up into the air, a graph of its height versus time traces out a parabola. At least, that is the conventional view, dating back to Newton. Einstein took the bold step of casting that notion aside and postulating that a massive body curves the coordinate system itself. Rather than following a curved path in a Cartesian coordinate system, the ball actually follows a "straight" path (a geodesic) in a curved coordinate system, returning to the thrower's hand at a later time because the geodesic leads it there. Gravity, therefore, is not really a force but is a manifestation of curvature in the geometry of spacetime. . .

. . . General relativity says that the geometrical curvature induced by a massive object does not arise everywhere instantaneously. Rather, it travels outward from its source at the speed of light. Thus, if a massive object alters its shape or orientation, or if a collection of objects changes its spatial arrangement, the gravitational effect—the curvature of spacetime—propagates away as a gravitational wave.

A gravitational wave may be described as a time-varying distortion of the geometry of space, temporarily altering the effective distance between any given pair of points. If the causative shift in mass is abrupt, the wave will take the form of a short pulse, much like the ripple produced after dropping a rock into a still pond. In the case of a periodic change, the wave will be sustained, much like the carrier wave for a broadcast radio signal. In either case, the amplitude of the wave will be inversely proportional to the distance from the source.

Unlike ordinary gravitational acceleration, which always points toward the source, a gravitational wave acts perpendicularly to the direction in which it is traveling, and thus is called a transverse wave. In this sense it is like light, rather than like sound, which propagates as longitudinal waves.

At any instant, a gravitational wave stretches space in one direction while shrinking it in the perpendicular direction. General relativity predicts two possible orientations for the stretching and shrinking, which physicists describe as two "polarization states." A given source may produce either one or a combination of both, depending on the particular motions of matter in directions transverse to the line of sight.

Any object encountered by a gravitational wave is stretched and shrunk along with the space in which it lives, and this is the basis for designing a detector. The key point is that the amplitude of a wave is described in physics terms by a strain, that is, a change in length per unit length. Thus, large objects will be affected more in an absolute sense than small objects.

Making Waves

Just what sorts of events generate gravitational waves? The short answer is big ones, where a lot of mass gets thrown around quickly. Indeed, the emission of gravitational radiation, being a relativistic effect, requires huge masses moving at velocities comparable to the speed of light. No man-made apparatus can produce gravitational waves large enough to be measured with any feasible instrument. The only possible sources are massive and energetic astrophysical systems. . .

. . . Compact binary systems have received much attention as gravitational-wave sources in part because the waveform of their emissions can be accurately modeled, at least for neutron stars and black holes with masses up to a few times the mass of the Sun. . .

. . . Astronomers hope that future measurements of gravitational waves will help to determine, for example, the abundance of binary neutron stars and other compact binary systems. Radio telescopes can detect such systems only if one of the objects is a pulsar. This limitation may explain why no observational information is yet available for binary systems containing a black hole and a neutron star, although such systems could be relatively abundant. Gravitational-wave astronomy should be able to detect these odd pairings as well as binary systems containing two black holes, something conventional astronomy would be hard-pressed to discern.

More ambitiously yet, cosmologists hope that gravitational waves might help to reveal how mass moved in the first moments after the Big Bang. The gravitational waves emitted at that time continue to bathe the Earth with tiny geometrical fluctuations, analogous to the cosmic microwave background radiation, but arising from much earlier in the evolution of the universe, at a time when the cosmos remained opaque to electromagnetic waves. . .

. . . Finally, physicists anticipate that this line of investigation will help to determine the true nature of gravity. General relativity, despite its spectacular success in various experimental tests, is not the only possible theory of gravity; others include so-called "scalar-tensor" theories, which, if valid, would have a direct influence on the nature of gravitational radiation. In particular, these theories predict that more than just two polarization states should be possible. Simultaneous observation of a reasonably strong source by multiple detectors would test these theories.

Although the scientific payoff promises to be enormous, direct detection of gravitational waves presents an extraordinary experimental challenge. The sources are expected to be either rare or intrinsically weak (or both). Consequently, the instruments must be very sensitive so that they can search a large volume of space in a reasonable amount of time. How sensitive? The amplitude of the strain expected from a typical gravitational wave reaching the Earth is about 10^{-21}. That number is so tiny it is hard to fathom. It means that the distance between two objects separated, say, by the diameter of the Earth would shrink and stretch only by an amount equal to the size of an atomic nucleus! . . .

Raising the Bar

The late Joseph Weber, a physicist at the University of Maryland, made the first serious attempts to measure gravitational waves in the 1960s. Weber's detector consisted of a large cylinder of solid aluminum, which was hung horizontally by a single wire around its middle. A sensitive transducer was placed at one end to measure vibrations of the cylinder at its resonant frequency, which could be induced by a passing gravitational wave. . .

. . . Bar detectors are highly sensitive only to a fairly narrow band of frequencies (near the resonant frequency of the bar), which limits the types of sources one can hope to detect with them. Therefore, in recent years the focus has shifted to interferometry, the use of light to measure precisely the distances between widely separated mirrors. Interferometers have the advantage of being sensitive to a comparatively broad range of frequencies.

Optical configurations differ somewhat, but all of these interferometers are variations on the basic design Albert A. Michelson used in 1881 and again six years later with the help of Edward Morley for the famous Michelson-Morley experiment. That test disproved the existence of the "ether," the ghostly medium that many 19th-century physicists believed must exist to account for the passage of light waves through space.

In outline, a gravitational-wave interferometer works as follows: A partially reflective mirror divides light from a laser into two beams, which then propagate along perpendicular arms of the device. Mirrors that are freely suspended at the ends of these arms reflect the two beams of light, returning them to a common point at the beam-splitting mirror. The output from this beam splitter depends on the relative phase of the waves in the two beams when they recombine, which in turn depends on how far each had to travel. Thus an interferometer can sensitively gauge the difference in length between the two arms down to a small fraction of the wavelength of light employed. . .

. . . Modern lasers, optics, photodetectors, and control systems permit vastly more stable and precise measurements than were available to Michelson and Morley. After decades of planning and prototyping, it is finally feasible to build large-scale interferometers capable of detecting the kinds of signals that might reasonably be reaching the Earth. . .

From Blueprints to Beams

LIGO, the Laser Interferometer Gravitational-Wave Observatory, represents the U.S. effort in the field. . . The LIGO Laboratory (a joint endeavor of the California Institute of Technology and the Massachusetts Institute of Technology, which manage the project) has observatory facilities at the Department of Energy's Hanford Site in Washington State and at Livingston, Louisiana.

Both installations contain a central building complex connected to two slender enclosures, which run for 4 kilometers in perpendicular directions. . . The Hanford Observatory has two independent interferometers, one with 4-kilometer arms and the other with 2-kilometer arms, which run side by side. Taken together, the three LIGO interferometers provide a powerful consistency check: The signal from a gravitational wave should appear in both Hanford detectors at the same time and with the same strain amplitude (that is, with a factor of two difference in absolute length change), and in the Livingston detector within the maximum light travel time between the two sites, 10 milliseconds earlier or later. . .

. . . There is a growing spirit of cooperation between LIGO investigators and those working with the three other gravitational-wave interferometers: GEO600 (a British-German project . . .), TAMA300 (a 300-meter interferometer . . . in Japan), and Virgo (a French-Italian interferometer . . .). Combining data from multiple interferometers makes it possible to perform further consistency checks and to test the fundamental properties of gravitational waves once a signal has been established.

Listening to the Universe

LIGO investigators conducted their first "science run" over a 17-day period in the summer of 2002 and followed that exercise with two more such sessions during 2003, each about two months long. . . We expect to reach design sensitivities next year, at which point we will begin collecting data more-or-less continuously. It is fitting that 2005 has been designated the World Year of Physics, with a particular emphasis on celebrating Einstein's revolutionary contributions to modern science. . .

. . . As a complement to ground-based detectors, gravitational waves can also be sought by precisely tracking the distance to an interplanetary spacecraft. Past experiments of this type have used a radio beacon beamed from Earth and retransmitted by the distant craft. Currently, the European Space Agency and NASA are collaborating to design the Laser Interferometer Space Antenna (LISA), a set of three spacecraft that will most likely be put into orbit around the Sun sometime in the next decade. This approach to gravitational-wave astronomy completely avoids the problems of ground motion and can accommodate arms millions of kilometers long, with laser beams propagating through the vacuum of space. LISA will scan a lower frequency band than LIGO can hope to cover and is targeting different sources. And unlike any of today's ground-based detectors, LISA will be sensitive enough to register gravitational waves from known sources . . . , which will provide valuable calibration standards for it.

Direct detection of gravitational waves is fantastically difficult, but decades of patient groundwork have brought us close to making it a reality. We look forward to finally sensing these minute ripples in spacetime in the not too distant future, and learning what they can tell us about distant astrophysical objects and about the nature of gravity itself.

Reprinted with permission from *American Scientist*, © 2004, Written by Peter S. Shawhan

Albert Einstein's general theory of relativity predicted in 1915 that when light passes near a very massive object, like our Sun, it would follow a straight line in the gravitationally caused curved space-time near the object. To an observer, it would appear as though the light was deflected by the massive object, a bending of light rays referred to as gravitational lensing. It was a triumph of Einstein's theory that the predicted light bending was observed in 1919, but the subject of light bending receded into the background after that. In 1979, however, gravitational lensing was rediscovered and has since become an important tool for astronomers to measure the size and age of the universe, as well as the distribution of matter and energy in it. Astronomers Leon V. E. Koopmans and Roger D. Blandford tell how gravitational lensing is used to determine the dark energy content of the universe, the dark matter content of the galaxy, and the location of black holes, for example. —LCK

From "Gravitational Lenses"
by Leon V. E. Koopmans and Roger D. Blandford
Physics Today, June 2004

Albert Einstein's general theory of relativity, completed in 1915, provided the tools needed to describe the universe's structure and to determine the propagation of light through it. It showed that if one pretends that spacetime has no curvature, then light would appear to be deflected as it passes by a gravitational potential well. Such bending—now called gravitational lensing—was seen for the first time during the solar eclipse of 29 May 1919 by British expeditions in Sobral, Brazil, and on Príncipe Island, off the west coast of Africa. The expeditions observed stars near the edge of the Sun and measured their displacement to be closer to Einstein's prediction of 1.7 arcseconds than to the Newtonian prediction of half that value. The 1919 measurements represented a major triumph for Einstein's theory.

For 60 years, the deflection of light by the Sun was the only known example of gravitational lensing. However, that changed in 1979 when Dennis Walsh, Bob Carswell, and Ray Weymann discovered a quasar that was multiply imaged by a massive foreground cluster galaxy.[1] Since then, the field of gravitational lensing has rapidly developed, both observationally and theoretically. Astronomers now use gravitational lensing to investigate the distribution of matter and energy in the universe from cosmological to stellar scales.

The Expanding Universe

The universe appears to be homogeneous and isotropic on its largest scales. And it is expanding. The history and future of its expansion are best captured by a single function, the scale factor $a(t)$, which is proportional to the mean separation of galaxies as a function of cosmic time (t).[2] It remains one of the main goals of observational cosmology to measure the scale factor accurately and to use the dynamical equations of motion governing cosmic expansion to infer the universe's material content.

A simple and natural cosmological model, inspired by inflation, posits that the spatial geometry of the universe is flat, not curved, and that a fraction Ω_m of its current total mass-energy density is in the form of predominantly cold matter—that is, matter that had near-zero speed at the onset of galaxy formation. The remaining fraction, $\Omega_\Lambda = 1 - \Omega_m$, is in the form of a constant dark energy density. The normalized first derivative of the scale factor $a/\mathring{a} \equiv H_0$ is the so-called Hubble constant. The "constant" actually changes with time, but throughout our discussion we'll use the Hubble constant's present-day value. The normalized second derivative $\ddot{a}/a = H_0^2(\Omega_m/2 - \Omega_\Lambda)$ measures the acceleration. Until a few years ago, cosmologists generally assumed the acceleration was negative due to the gravitational pull of matter. In fact, the opposite is the case: The acceleration is positive—prima facie evidence for the existence of a dark-energy component with negative pressure, which produces a negative active gravitational mass. . .

Measuring the Hubble Constant

The constant H_0 is one of the most important parameters in physical cosmology, because it indicates both the size and the age of the universe. However, measuring the Hubble constant has been plagued by difficulties ever since the 1920s, when astronomers discovered that the universe is expanding.

The classic approach has been to construct a so-called cosmic distance ladder: Astronomers use nearby celestial objects, for which distances are easier to

measure, to calibrate the distances to objects that are
farther away. In that manner, they can build up distances
to far-off objects that effectively move with the Hubble
flow—that is, the average speed with which galaxies
would recede from us in a completely homogeneous and
isotropic universe. Astronomers, though, have only a
poor understanding of the underlying physics of many

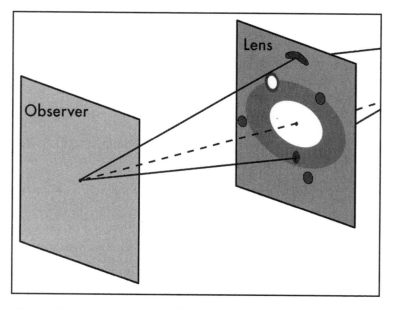

Figure 1. Strong gravitational lens geometry. Light emitted from a
source travels along multiple geodesic paths—two in the case
illustrated—to an observer who sees multiple distorted images of the
source projected on the sky. The two paths have different lengths, and
so a geometric time delay is introduced between the images. That the
paths also sample different portions of the gravitational potential
leads to an additional time delay, sometimes called a Shapiro delay.
Astronomers measure the sum of the two time delays, which is
inversely proportional to the Hubble constant. The lens illustrated here
is a galaxy with stars *(light gray)* and a surrounding dark-matter
(dark gray) halo. Also shown are several small dwarf satellites, with
and without luminous matter, that can affect the lensed images.

of the objects used in constructing the distance ladder. Thus, the empirical corrections they apply to observed data can hide biases that limit the reliability of results obtained using the classic ladder approach.

Gravitational lenses promise an accurate, independent measurement of the Hubble constant in a single step. The idea, as first proposed by Sjur Refsdal in 1964[5] is to observe a multiply imaged variable source. Lenses that yield multiple images, such as the one shown in figure 1, are called strong. The total travel times associated with the different images created by strong lenses can differ by days or even years and are inversely proportional to H_o. Such time delays are ideally suited to accurate measurement by ground-based radio and optical telescopes in dedicated monitoring programs. The physics of gravitational lensing is well understood. Moreover, astronomers can carry out lensing measurements on relatively nearby sources, which allows them to determine a value for the Hubble constant that does not strongly depend on such cosmological parameters as Ω_m and Ω_Λ. . .

Constraining Cosmologies

The number of strong lenses one expects to see in a large lens survey can be predicted as a function of the geometry and kinematics of the universe, provided one has adequate knowledge of the redshift distribution of the lensed sources, the local density of the lens galaxies, and the mass-density profiles of the lenses. When one varies cosmological parameters, the volume between Earth and a distribution of distant sources changes. Consequently, so does the number of inferred intermediate lens galaxies.

For example, increasing the dark energy increases the volume and thus the number of gravitational lenses one would expect to see in a survey. By comparing model predictions with results from lens surveys, astronomers can constrain cosmological parameters.

A different kind of technique, which is sensitive to the matter density of the universe, relies on weak gravitational lensing. That is, it relies on lensing not strong enough to form multiple images. The gravitational potential variations of weak lenses cause small distortions in the shapes of background sources. By measuring those distortions, one can determine the amplitude of density fluctuations. So-called tomographic surveys give three-dimensional information; otherwise, one determines 2D variations in which the radial coordinate is essentially integrated out. The current weak-lensing measurements are degenerate in that a measurement might be consistent with small fluctuations in a high-density universe or large fluctuations in a low-density universe. But microwave background observations uniquely determine the density fluctuations at early times: By combining microwave-background and weak-lensing observations, one can determine the mass-energy density of the universe.

Both strong and weak lensing give values of Ω_m significantly less than 1. The largest strong lens survey—CLASS—gives $\Omega_m \approx 0.2$–0.3 with an error of about 0.1, assuming a flat geometry.[7] The current weak-lensing determination gives an m of about 0.3 with 10 % error.[8] Those results are in good agreement with independent determinations from, for example, distant supernovae. . .

. . . The nature and behavior of the mass fluctuations are also of interest in their own right. After all, structures such as clusters, galaxies, and stars originated from some sort of fluctuation, and those structures grow and evolve under the influence of their own gravity. Weak and strong gravitational lensing both provide valuable tools for measuring the mass distribution in the universe—from the largest scales to the smallest.[9] Because the deflection of light does not depend on the nature or dynamical state of the deflecting mass or energy, one can investigate the distribution of all mass including, particularly, the dark matter. Gravitational-lensing approaches are thus superior to galaxy-distribution studies that only trace luminous matter and hence need to be supplemented with an uncertain prescription, called bias, that allows one to relate light fluctuations to matter fluctuations. Bias, in other words, is a rule for determining where galaxies form in a sea of dark matter. . .

Stars and Planets

Relatively small masses can be detected using micro-lensing, the production of flux changes in compact background sources due to the passage of intervening compact lenses close to the line of sight. Microlensing forms multiple images and may be viewed as strong lensing on very small angular scales, typically micro- to milliarcseconds. Present-day telescopes cannot resolve the multiple images at such small scales; rather, they detect changes in the total brightness of the lensed source.

Both luminous stars and compact dark objects can serve as microlenses. The probability that a specified background source is lensed by the foreground stellar population of the Milky Way is tiny—something like 10^{-6}—so observers must conduct large microlensing surveys. They look either near the center of the Milky Way or toward large nearby galaxies, where millions of stars have the potential to be lensed.

The most interesting results have come from the Massive Compact Halo Object and Expérience de Recherche d'Objets Sombres teams, which monitored stars in the Large Magellanic Cloud and attempted to find rapid magnification changes due to compact dark matter in our galactic halo.[15] The MACHO team claims that about 20% of the Milky Way halo consists of compact objects of some 0.5 solar mass. That mass content is greater than the total mass of the known stars. Self-lensing, in which both the source and lens are in the Magellanic Clouds, is likely to be the explanation of the MACHO results. The EROS team finds fewer microlensing events than the MACHO team and sets an upper limit of 25% for the compact dark matter content of the halo. In any event, it is now clear that only a small fraction of the Milky Way halo's dark matter consists of massive compact objects and that dark matter must be sought in the particle physics domain.

Microlensing is also invaluable as a probe of black holes. One recognizes a potential "dark star" when a lens mass is measured to be more than about 3 solar masses, too heavy to be a neutron star or white dwarf. If the lens is close enough, one might be able to rule out a luminous star as an explanation, which would leave only a black hole as a viable candidate. The microlensing technique is pretty much the only tool astronomers have for measuring the density of single black holes in the Milky Way. It has already been used to find three reasonably convincing black hole candidates.

A binary lens yields a more complex flux distribution. Such complex light curves could be a good way to identify planets that are far too faint to be seen directly—the planet and its star are the imaged binary. The first convincing case of a microlensing event by a star with a Jupiter-mass companion has recently been found by the Optical Gravitational Lensing Experiment and Microlensing Observations in Astrophysics collaborations.[16]

Microlensing is improbable in our galaxy, but stars in more distant strong-lensing galaxies can form caustic networks that can magnify or demagnify compact sources on microarcsecond scales.[17] The accretion disks in lensed optical quasars or the shock fronts in lensed radio jets, for example, could be highly magnified; one could then probe their size and structure on extremely small angular scales. From microlensing studies, astronomers have learned that massive black holes contribute only a small percentage of the mass in distant galactic halos.

Large and Deep Surveys

The rapid transformation of gravitational lensing from a scientific curiosity to a cosmological tool has been made possible by painstaking observations at mostly radio and optical wavelengths. However, much work remains to be done—observable stars and galaxies number over a hundred billion.

The next steps are already in progress. Large and deep surveys now being carried out with ground-based telescopes will observe more than 10 million galaxies and measure their weak-lensing distortions on an angular scale of about a degree. They should also discover many new cases of strong lensing and microlensing. Some of those surveys will be able to determine the distances of the galaxies using galactic photometric redshifts—essentially colors—and thus enable tomographic studies. The ongoing surveys will provide data on the evolution of mass fluctuations. The data can then be compared against simulations that make accurate predictions as a function of a given cosmological model. . .

Scientists have only partly been able to script the study of lensing; the history of the field is full of unanticipated phenomena. What better place to seek further serendipitous discoveries than in observational investigations of dark energy, dark matter, dark stars, and planets? It is in the unscripted discoveries, we predict, that gravitational lensing will continue to contribute most to the understanding of the universe.

End Notes

1. D. Walsh, R. F. Carswell, R. J. Weymann, *Nature* **279**, 381 (1979) [INSPEC].
2. Further details can be found in any good cosmology textbook. See, for example, J. A. Peacock, *Cosmological Physics*, Cambridge U. Press, New York (1999).
5. S. Refsdal, *Mon. Not. R. Astron. Soc.* **128**, 307 (1964).
7. K-H Chae *et al.*, *Phys. Rev. Lett.* **89**, 151301 (2002) [SPIN].
8. C. R. Contaldi, H. Hoekstra, A. Lewis, *Phys. Rev. Lett.* **90**, 221303 (2003) [SPIN].
9. See, for example, P. Schneider, < http://arXiv.org/abs/astro-ph/0306465 > .
15. See, for example, N. W. Evans, < http://arXiv.org/abs/astro-ph/0304252 > .
16. I. A. Bond *et al.*, < http://arXiv.org/abs/astro-ph/0404309 > .
17. R. Kayser, S. Refsdal, R. Stabel, *Astron. Astrophys.* **166**, 36 (1986).

Web Sites

Due to the changing nature of Internet links, the Rosen Publishing Group, Inc., has developed an online list of Web sites related to the subject of this book. This site is updated regularly. Please use this link to access the list:

http://www.rosenlinks.com/cdfp/gemf

For Further Reading

Bromley, Allan D. *A Century of Physics*. New York, NY: Springer-Verlag Publishers, 2002.

Chabay, Ruth, and Bruce Sherwood. *Matter & Interactions I: Modern Mechanics* and *Matter & Interactions II: Electric & Magnetic Interactions*. New York, NY: John Wiley & Sons, 2002.

Ehrlich, Robert. *Nine Crazy Ideas in Science: A Few Might Even Be True*. Princeton, NJ: Princeton University Press, 2001.

Fritzsch, H. (translated from German by K. Heusch). *The Curvature of Spacetime: Newton, Einstein, and Gravitation*. New York, NY: Columbia University Press, 2002.

Rakov, Vladimir A., and Martin A. Uman. *Lightning: Physics and Effects*. Cambridge, MA: Cambridge University Press, 2003.

Ratner, Mark A., and Daniel Ratner. *Nanotechnology: A Gentle Introduction to the Next Big Idea*. Upper Saddle River, NJ: Prentice Hall Press, 2002.

Saslow, Wayne M. *Concepts Before Equations— Electricity, Magnetism, and Light*. New York, NY: Academic Press, 2002.

Bibliography

The American Institute of Physics Bulletin of Physics News. "Physics News Update." Retrieved October 19, 2004 (http://www.aip.org/physnews/update).

Bishop, David, Peter Gammel, and C. Randy Giles. "The Little Machines That Are Making It Big." *Physics Today*, October 2001, p. 38.

Dvali, Georgi. "Out of the Darkness." *Scientific American*, February 2004, p. 68.

Feder, Barnaby J. "The Biggest Jolt to Power Since Franklin Flew His Kite." *New York Times*, April 27, 2004.

Feng, Jonathan L. "Searching for Gravity's Hidden Strength." *Science*, October 31, 2003, p. 795.

Forrest, Stephen R. "The Path to Ubiquitous and Low-Cost Organic Electronic Appliances on Plastic." *Nature*, April 29, 2004, p. 911.

Gassmann, Fritz, Rüdiger Kötz, and Alexander Wokaun. "Supercapacitors Boost the Fuel Cell Car." *Europhysics News*, September/October 2003, p. 176.

Horne, Keith. "Gravitational Lensing Brings Extrasolar Planets into Focus." *Physics World*, June 2004, p. 19.

Horowitz, Paul, and Winfield Hill. *The Art of Electronics*. Second edition. Cambridge, MA: Cambridge University Press, 1989.

Howard, Webster E. "Better Organic Displays with Organic Films." *Scientific American*, February 2004, p. 76.

Koltsov, Denis, and Mark Perry. "Magnets and Nanometres: Mutual Attraction." *Physics World*, July 2004, p. 31.

Koopmans, Leon V. E., and Roger D. Blandford. "Gravitational Lenses." *Physics Today*, June 2004, p. 45.

Leary, Warren E. "New Satellites to Map Gravity." *New York Times*, March 19, 2002.

Lerner, Eric J. "What's Wrong with the Electric Grid?" *Industrial Physicist*, October/November 2003, p. 8.

Lorenzini, Enrico, and Juan Sanmartín. "Electrodynamic Tethers in Space." *Scientific American*, August 2004, p. 50.

Lucent Technologies. "The Transistor." Retrieved October 19, 2004 (http://www.lucent.com/minds/transistor/index.html).

Malsch, Ineke. "Tiny Tips Probe Nanotechnology." *Industrial Physicist*, October/November 2002, p. 16.

Marder, Michael P. *Condensed Matter Physics*. Hoboken, NJ: Wiley-Interscience, 2000.

Merlino, Robert L., and John A. Goree. "Dusty Plasmas in the Laboratory, Industry, and Space." *Physics Today*, July 2004, p. 32.

Paul, Clayton R., Keith W. Whites, and Syed A Nasar. *Introduction to Electromagnetic Fields*. Third edition. Boston, MA: WCB/McGraw-Hill, 1998.

Pelrine, Ronald E. "Diamagnetic Levitation." *American Scientist*, September/October 2004.

Perl, Martin. "Fraction Man." *New Scientist*, June 21, 2003, p. 44.

Schechter, Bruce. "Ghost in the Machine." *New Scientist*, May 29, 2004, p. 38.

Schwartz, John. "Free from Gravity, These Students Taste Outer Space." *New York Times*, June 8, 2004, p. F3.

Senturia, Stephen D. "Microsystem Design." New York, NY: Kluwar Academic Publishers, 2001.

Shawhan, Peter S. "Gravitational Waves and the Effort to Detect Them." *American Scientist*, July/August 2004, p. 350.

Solin, Stuart A. "Magnetic Field Nanosensors." *Scientific American*, July 2004, p. 71.

Thomas, John E., and Michael E. Gehm "Optically Trapped Fermi Gases." *American Scientist*, May/June 2004, p. 238.

Topinka, Mark A., Robert M. Westervelt, and Eric J. Heller. "Imaging Electron Flow." *Physics Today*, December 2003, p. 47.

Weissman, John H. "Geomagnetic Flip." *Physics World*, April 2004, p. 31.

Weisstein, Eric. "Eric Weisstein's World of Physics." Retrieved October 19, 2004 (http://scienceworld. wolfram.com/physics/).

Index

A

Alfvén, Hannes, 147–148
American Physical Society
    ("Woodstock of physics"),
    131, 134
Ampère, André-Marie, 6
Anderson localisation, 22, 23
Anderson, Philip, 21
    "gang of four" research team,
    21–22

B

Barry, Dr. Daniel T., 169
Binnig, Gerd, 92, 93
bismuth, 135
blackout of August 14, 2003, 40,
    47–48
Bloch, Felix, 21
Blandford, Roger D., 189
Bose-Einstein condensate, 98, 99,
    106, 107
Braunbeck, Werner, 140

C

Carreras, Ben, 46
Carswell, Bob, 190
Casazza, John, 41, 45, 49
Casimir, H. B. G., 7, 114
Casimir force, 7, 113, 114–115
Cavendish, Henry, 6, 8, 9
CEN/STAR, 95
ceramic superconductors
    (high temperature
    superconductivity)
    discovery of, 131

explanation of, 133–134
    obstacles in developments,
        134–135, 136
charge carrier transport, 124–125
Chu, Steven, 102
Clarke, Arthur C., 62
Collicott, Steven H., 167
composite boson, 106
composite fermion, 106, 107
conductivity theory, contra-
    dictions to, 20–21, 24, 27
Cooper pairs, 24–25
Cornell, Eric, 98, 107
Coulomb, Charles, 6

D

de Broglie wavelength, 103–105
diamagnetic levitation
    explanation of, 140–142
    first demonstration of, 140
    lack of exploration in, 142–143
    uses of, 144–145
diamagnetic materials
    explanation of, 139–140, 141
    uses of, 137, 140
Dirac, P. A. M., 105
dusty plasma
    characteristics of, 153
    experiments with, 155–156
    explanation of, 146, 147
    and fusion plasma, 152
    and particulate contamination,
        150–152
    and Saturn's rings, 146–147,
        148–150

E

Earnshaw's Theorem, 138, 140
Einstein, Albert, general theory of
    relativity, 181–182, 189, 190
electrical conductivity, 20
electricity
    deregulation of, 42, 45
    explanation of, 40, 41–44
    solutions for, 48–50
electrodynamic tether (EDT)
    benefits of, 62–63, 66, 68–71
    explanation of, 61–63
    problems of, 67, 73
electromagnetism
    applications of, 5–6
    forces of, 6
    study of, 6
Expérience de Recherche d'Objets
    Sombres, 196
extraordinary magneto
    resistance (EMR)
    applications of, 75, 76, 82–86
    and computer disk drives, 83–85
    discovery of, 75–76
    explanation of, 74–75, 77–82
    and semiconductor superlattice,
    75–76

F

Faraday, Michael, 6, 20
Feder, Barnaby J., 131
Federal Energy Regulatory
    Commission's (FERC) Order
    888, criticism of, 45–47
Feng, Jonathan L., 172
Fermi, Enrico, 105
Fermi gas, creation of, 98–99,
    103, 107
Feynman, Richard, 109, 110
Forrest, Stephen R., 119
fractional electric charges, 7,
    10–11
    research findings, 15, 18
    research for, 13–18

research team, 15
theories on, 12
Franklin, Benjamin, 6

G

Gassman, Fritz, 50
Gehm, Michael E., 97
Goertz, Christoph, 149–150
Goldman, Allen, 24
Goree, John, 146
gravitational lensing
    applications of, 193–195
    field of, 190, 197–198
    microlensing, 195–197
gravitational wave
    applications of discovery, 184
    causes of, 183
    characteristics of, 182–183
    experiments in, 185–188
    research challenges, 184–185
gravity
    detectors of large extra
        dimensions, 177–178
    search for large extra
        dimensions, 175–177
    weakness of, 173–174
Gravity Recovery and Climate
    Experiment (Grace)
    explanation of, 161
    goals of, 161, 162
    gravity maps, 162–164
    Tom and Jerry satellites, 160, 163

H

Hayes, Gregory W., 166
Heisenberg uncertainty
    principle, 25–26, 98–99
Heller, Eric, 28
Hill, Jay, 149
Hubble constant, measuring of,
    191–193
Hulet, Randy, 107

I

International Space Station, 61, 156

J

Jin, Deborah, 107
Jones, Gareth, 16

K

Karnes, Rebecca, 168
Ketterle, Wolfgang, 98, 107
Koch, N. F. H. von, 59
Koopmans, Leon V. E., 189
Kötz, Rüdiger, 50, 55
Kravchenko, Sergey, 22–23
  criticism of experiments, 23
  metallic experiments, 22–23

L

Langmuir, Irving, 147
Laser Interferometer Gravitational-
  Wave Observatory (LIGO),
  186–188
Leary, Warren E., 159
Lenz's Law, 140

M

macroscopic quantum systems,
  creating of, 99–103
magnetic materials, 139
Massive Compact Halo Object, 196
Maxwell's fundamental
  equations, 138
Mendis, Asoka, 149
Merlino, Robert, 146
metals, properties of, 21
Meyer, Ernst, 94–95
Michelson, Albert A., 185
microelectromechanical systems
  (MEMS), 7
  applications of, 108–109
  in automotive devices, 111–112
  in magnetometers, 113–114
  in micromechanics, 115–118
  production of, 110–111
  in scientific measurements,
    112–113
microscopic black holes, 176–177

N

Millikan, Robert, oil drop exper-
  iments of, 7, 10, 11, 13, 14
Morfill, Greg, 149–150
Morley, Edward, 185

N

NASA (National Aeronautics and
  Space Administration) KC-135
  program
attracting students, 166–167
experiences of, 165–166,
  169–170, 171–172
reaction to, 167–168, 170–172
Nefedov, Anatoli, 156
Newton, Isaac
  central inverse-square force
    law, 172
  law of universal gravitation,
    8, 161
  *Philosophiae Naturalis Principia
    Mathematica*, 8

O

Oersted, Hans Christian, 6
organic thin-film materials
  applications of, 125–127
  benefits of, 120–122, 126–128
  biological materials, 122, 123–124
  development of, 119, 120–121
  excitonic state, 124
  Frenkel exciton, 124
  interest in, 120, 121
  polymers, 122, 123, 124, 128
  "small molecule" (monomers),
    122–123, 124

P

Pashkin, Yu. A., 85
Perl, Martin, 11
Pelrine, Ronald E., 137
perturbation theory, 23
Peterson, Dr. Dean, 136
Phillips, Philip, 19, 20, 23, 25,
  26, 27
plasma, 146, 153–154

Pohl, D. W., 92
Polder, D., 7
Priestly, Joseph, 6
Purdue project, 168

R

Reeves, Dr. Jodi L., 133
Refsdal, Sjur, 193
Rohrer, Heinrich, 92

S

Salomon, Christophe, 107
scanning probe microscopes (SPMs)
    atomic force microscope
        (AFM), 89, 90–91, 93–94, 95
    friction force microscope (FFM),
        89, 94–95
    magnetic force microscope
        (MFM), 89, 95
    scanning near-field optical micro-
        scope (SNOM), 90, 92–93
    scanning tunneling microscope
        (STM), 28, 90, 92
Schwartz, John, 165
Selvamanickam, Dr. Venkat, 134
Shawhan, Peter S., 179
Spitzer, Lyman, 147
Stanford Linear Accelerator
    Center (SLAC), 10, 11, 12
Stillman, Lester, 81, 82
supercapacitors
    benefits of, 50, 51–52, 53–55
    developments of, 55
    explanation of, 52–53, 56–57
superconductivity
    contradictions to theory, 24–25
    developments in, 132–133
    discovery of, 132
    theory of, 24
    uses of, 140
Swenson, Charles M., 170

T

Tapley, Dr. Byron D., 161–162
Tethered Satellite System (TSS), 67

Thomas, John E., 97
Toole, Loren, 46
Topinka, Mark, 28, 33
Tsai, J. Shen, 85
Tsiolkovsky, Konstantin, 62
two-dimensional electron gas
    (2DEG)
    behaviors of, 31
    and electron transport, 30
    experiments with, 29–30
    imaging of, 30–31, 32–37
    imaging findings, 36–38
    production of, 29
    and quantum Hall effect
        (QHE), 31

U

universe, expansion of, 190–191

V

van der Waals forces, 121
Ventre, Brian, 167
Versailles Project on Advanced
    Materials and Standards
    (VAMAS), 95, 96

W

Walsh, Dennis, 190
Watkins, Dr. Michael, 160, 161,
    163, 164
Weber, Joseph, 185
Westervelt, Robert, 28, 33
Weymann, Ray, 190
Wieman, Carl, 98, 107
Wokaun, Alexander, 50
Wolf, Charles, 81, 82
world line, 181

Y

YBCO, 135, 136
Yurek, Dr. Gregory J., 134, 135

Z

Zammit, Adrianna, 170
Zimanyi, Gergely, 23

About the Editor

Cindy Krysac, Ph.D., is a physics researcher, writer, and teacher with more than ten years of experience teaching students at the undergraduate level. After receiving her Ph.D. in physics from the University of Toronto, she has been a postdoctoral researcher at Pennsylvania State University, in State College, Pennsylvania, and an Assistant Professor at the University of the Pacific in Stockton, California, where she taught upper division electromagnetism and the physics of music for several years. Her research focuses on the physics of fracture. She is currently on sabbatical in Toronto, Canada, writing science articles and working on several writing projects.

Photo Credits

Front cover (clockwise from top right): "Infinite Textures," © Comstock Images Royalty free division; "Electron Flow" © Eric Heller/Photo Researchers, Inc.; "Liquid Crystal," © Getty Images; background image of gyroscope © Getty Images; portrait, Isaac Newton © Library of Congress, Prints and Photographs Division. Back cover: top image "Electrons Orbiting Nucleus" © Royalty-Free/ Corbis; bottom: Liquid Crystal © Getty Images.

Designer: Geri Fletcher; Editor: Joann Jovinelly